For

Elizabeth H. Abraham

with best wishes

Beatrice Smith

A Painted Herbarium

"Who knows but you may hear of me as an artist yet."
—Emily Hitchcock, 1866

The University of Minnesota Press
gratefully acknowledges
the generous assistance provided
for the publication of this book
by Mrs. Reuel D. Harmon
and the
Margaret S. Harding Memorial Endowment
honoring the first director of the
University of Minnesota Press

Emily Hitchcock Terry

BEATRICE SCHEER SMITH

A Painted Herbarium

THE LIFE AND ART OF
EMILY HITCHCOCK TERRY (1838–1921)

Beatrice Scheer Smith

UNIVERSITY OF MINNESOTA PRESS

MINNEAPOLIS / LONDON

*Published by the University of Minnesota Press
2037 University Avenue Southeast, Minneapolis, MN 55414
Printed in Japan on acid-free paper*

*Photo, page iv: Emily Hitchcock Terry, ca. 1885–90.
(Photograph by E. A. Record, Saratoga, New York.
Smith College Archives, Smith College.)*

Jacket and book design by Diane Gleba Hall

Library of Congress Cataloging-in-Publication Data

Smith, Beatrice S.
*A painted herbarium: the life and art of Emily Hitchcock Terry,
1838–1921 / Beatrice Scheer Smith.*
p.   cm.
Includes bibliographical references and index.
ISBN 0-8166-2153-5
1. Terry, Emily Hitchcock, 1838–1921.   2. Botanical artists—
United States—Biography.   3. Botanists—United States—Biography.
4. Botanical illustration—Minnesota—History. I. Title.
QK98.183.T37S55 1992
581'.022'S—dc20
[B]

92-274
CIP

*The University of Minnesota is an
equal-opportunity educator and employer.*

To my first professor of botany
EDMUND W. SINNOTT
who changed the course of my life

Contents

Acknowledgments

"COLLECTING IS A WORLD HABIT," WROTE ARNOLD Bennett, the English novelist and dramatist. He explained: "Collectors practise it consciously and with a definite, recognized aim. The rest of us practise it more or less unconsciously." A notable example of the collector at work is the hero of our day, the scientist: in addition to things of innumerable sorts, he or she collects ideas and facts with which to support or refute hypotheses. To the conscious collectors with their defined aims and goals, to the devoted *amateurs,* and indeed to the unconscious collectors, who may be merely accumulators—they just save things—we owe an enormous debt of gratitude. Because of them we can ferret out who we were and who we are. In their vast accumulations of saved things and recorded thoughts we find ourselves.

Among researchers none is more beholden to the savers of the past than the delver into history. Buried in endless collections lie the answers to many of our questions, just waiting to be discovered. The process of discovery would soon come to a grinding halt, however, if in fact this process could ever begin, without the people who put and keep these collections in order and thus make the information they hold retrievable. To find one photograph among a hundred, one letter among a thousand, one scientific paper among several thousand, one book among several hundred thousand, one herbarium specimen among a million—these are the tasks that face the librarian, the curator, the archivist. The historical researcher is totally dependent not only on the savers of the past, but also on the skill of the present-day guardians of the collections they amassed.

The study of Emily Hitchcock Terry is a preeminent example of the dependence of the investigator on things saved and on those who preside over them. Emily Terry saved her paintings and pressed plants; in fact, her mother before her did likewise. Letters were saved, as were college records; newspapers; histories of organizations and proceedings of societies, large and small, prominent and obscure; photographs; scientific journals and books; legal documents, records of our living and dying; and other items too numerous to mention. To the people of the past who made these collections, to George Davenport and Walter Deane, who saved literally thousands of letters, I acknowledge my indebtedness; and to those of the present I express my thanks, not only for taking care of laboriously assembled collections and for willingly and skillfully finding in them the things I knew were there, but also for putting me in touch with countless things I did not know were there. Only because of these complex networks of preserved materials and the historically minded people who superintend them can the story of Emily Hitchcock Terry be told.

I first became acquainted with, and later studied, Emily Terry's book of paintings at the Arcadia Nature Center and Wildlife Sanctuary in Easthampton, Massachusetts, where the volume was housed from 1973 to 1991. Mary Shanley, director of the center, graciously granted me permission to examine the paintings and study them in detail. Hazel Palmer, librarian, who answered my first inquiry about the Terry book, and Jane Layton, assistant director, facilitated my visits to the center and arranged a work space, for which I thank them.

I want to recognize with gratitude the significant contributions of three people with reference to the Terry paintings. Of prime importance was the generous permission on behalf of Smith College of Ruth Mortimer, curator of rare books at the Smith College Library, Northampton, Massachusetts, to reproduce the Emily Terry paintings. Terry presented her volume of paintings to the college in 1913, where it is now housed. Our pleasure in this study of Terry's life and art would be significantly diminished without examples of Terry's work. Second, Dr. C. John Burk, Gates Professor in the Biological Sciences and curator of the herbarium at Smith College, made possible the initial photography of the paintings. His cooperation greatly simplified my task, and his help in this and other ways moved the project forward substantially. Just as important to me were his sustained interest in the Terry study and his belief in its value. And last, but not least in this triumvirate of people, is Dr. Gerald B. Ownbey, professor emeritus of botany at the University of Minnesota. I thank him for his painstaking examination of the paintings and his work in verifying, and in some cases correcting, Terry's plant identifications. His expertise was indispensable to my accuracy, and his ability to make specific adjustments in nomenclature on the basis of his study of the paintings is a high tribute to the quality of Emily Terry's botanical art.

Special thanks are due the following people, who made available particularly significant materials from collections in their institutions. The core of the project developed from information they supplied: Drs. Hollis G. Bedell and Jean Boise Cargill, archivists, Library of the Gray Herbarium, Harvard University; Maida Goodwin, archives specialist, Smith College Archives; Patricia J. Albright, college history/ archives librarian, Mount Holyoke College Archives Collection; and Daria D'Arienzo, archivist of the college, Amherst College Library.

I pay tribute to the librarians at several excellent Minnesota libraries, who always offered efficient and knowledgeable assistance: Ramsey County Public Library, Roseville; Minnesota Historical Society Reference Library, St. Paul; the various libraries of the University of Minnesota, particularly the St. Paul Campus Central Library; Minneapolis Public Library; and St. Paul Public Library. Their skill at tracking down obscure references, finding rare materials, and arranging interlibrary loans for unusual items was noteworthy.

My travels in the course of researching Emily Terry's life took me to Dorset, Vermont, where Terry experienced her happiest days in botany. My thanks go to the following Dorset people who made it possible for me to fill in some of the details of Terry's post-Minnesota life. Elisabeth B. Sturges, former president of the Dorset Historical Society, answered my first inquiry about Terry and was instrumental in locating Terry's long-since-forgotten fern herbarium sheets. Arthur W. Gilbert, whose father collected plants with Emily Terry, welcomed me to his home and showed me Terry's ferns. William H. Manley, curator of the Dorset Historical Society, who discovered a second set of Terry's ferns among the society's collections, provided me with illustrations and essential facts about the town of Dorset and its environs.

I acknowledge with gratitude the contributions of several individuals, recognizing full well that their encouraging interest in Emily Terry was equally as important as the material assistance they provided: Dr. Eugene C. Worman, Jr., whose study of Emily Hitchcock Terry's mother, Orra White Hitchcock, first made me aware of the Terry paintings; Anna-Marie Ettel, who brought the Worman study to my attention; Penelope Krosch, University of Minnesota archivist, who set me on the path of Cassius Terry and his connection with George Armstrong Custer; Daniel Lombardo, curator of special collections at The Jones Library, Inc., Amherst, Massachusetts; Dr. David S. Barrington, curator and professor, Pringle Herbarium, the University of Vermont, Burlington; Michael Heinz, researcher of early plant exploration in Minnesota; James Keith, historian, Macalester-Plymouth Church, St. Paul; Anne A. Hage, archivist, The Minnesota Conference, United Church of Christ, Minneapolis; Dr. G. B. Morey, professor and associate director, Minnesota Geological Survey, University of Minnesota, who furnished details about Cassius Terry's work with the survey and enhanced my understanding of scientific exploration in Minnesota during the latter part of the nineteenth century; and Sylvia and Herbert Lewthwaite, my companions in exploring Emily Terry's New England. Space prohibits mentioning individually all those people who were valuable sources of support simply because they listened with good grace—over and over—to my progress reports on the Terry research. They will remember hours of conversation, which frequently helped clarify my own thinking, and will know that this expression of gratitude includes them all.

Finally, a group of people at the University of Minnesota Press managed the transformation of a manuscript and a package of illustrations into a book: Lisa Freeman, director of the press; Kathy Wolter, production and design manager; Barbara A. Coffin, editor; and Mary Byers, copy editor. Together with Diane Gleba Hall, designer, they brought the project to fruition. Their enthusiasm for it never waned.

In conclusion, a special word of recognition and thanks is due Peggy Harmon, a lover of wildflowers, whose financial assistance made possible the realization of the undertaking. Because of Peggy Harmon's generosity, Terry's plant portraits, heretofore unpublished and known to only a few, can be enjoyed by flower lovers everywhere, now and into the future. We are all grateful to her.

B. S. S.

A Painted Herbarium

Prologue

"I AM NOW TAKING LESSONS IN DRAWING AND PAINT-
ing in Cooper Institute, and intend to continue
here through the year, and study nature afterwards. Who knows but you may hear of me as an artist
yet?" Thus, in 1866, Emily Hitchcock revealed her hopes
for the future in an alumnae newsletter to her fellow members of the class of 1859 at Mary Lyon's Mount Holyoke
Female Seminary in South Hadley, Massachusetts (now
Mount Holyoke College).[1]

But art was not the only compelling interest in Emily
Hitchcock Terry's life. We know of at least one other: the
science of botany. That she considered herself a serious,
qualified student of botany she made clear in a letter to a
new botanical colleague:

> My father was Edward Hitchcock the Geologist. My
> brother, of the same name was the Father of physical cul-
> ture, familiarly known as "Old Doc" during a fifty year
> Professorship at Amherst, and he died three years ago. My
> other brother, Charles by name, was Professor of Geology
> at Dartmouth College for fifty years—or about that, and
> he is now living in Honolulu. We two are the last survivors

of our family. You may have known of them. My father was a botanist as well as a geologist, and he taught me botany.

You will pardon the personal information, but I wanted you to know that tho I am now a Terry, yet I can lay claim to belong to a well-known scientific family, by the name of Hitchcock.[2]

Terry's interests in art and science merged and found their most significant expression in a group of forty-nine watercolor paintings of the flora of Minnesota, principally wildflowers, most of them done between 1875 and 1878. They are part of a larger collection, titled *American Flowers*—142 paintings in all, made in various locations from 1850 to 1910. The paintings, known to only a few and virtually unnoticed for more than a hundred years, were presented by Terry to the Department of Botany of Smith College, Northampton, Massachusetts, in 1913.

Emily Hitchcock Terry lived in Minnesota only twelve years—from 1872 to 1884—but long enough to produce a body of work that, now recognized, not only fulfills her wish to be "heard of" as an artist, but also establishes her as one of the earliest illustrators of Minnesota's plants, perhaps even the earliest. In addition, her plant collections in the state from various widely separated localities are noted frequently by Upham in his 1884 catalogue of the flora of Minnesota.[3] The excitement of the realization that Upham's plant collector Mrs. E. H. Terry of St. Paul, Minnesota, and Emily Hitchcock Terry, botanical artist of Amherst and Northampton, Massachusetts, were one and the same was exceeded only by the excitement of the discovery that many of the paintings in her collection were done from nature in Minnesota. The story of this Massachusetts woman and her stressful, but nevertheless creative and productive, brief sojourn in Minnesota is told on the following pages.

The Early Years
1838–1859

THE YOUNGEST OF THE SIX SURVIVING CHILDREN OF Edward and Orra White Hitchcock, Emily was born in Amherst, Massachusetts, on 9 November 1838. She was a fortunate blending of the capabilities of her two highly intellectual and artistic parents.[1]

Emily's father, Edward Hitchcock, educated at Yale University in theology and science, first held a pastorate in a Congregational church, but soon found himself more at home in the sciences, foremost among them geology. He has been called the father of American geology, but his scientific curiosity extended to other branches of science including chemistry and natural history, especially botany. He held a professorship in chemistry and natural history in Amherst College for twenty years (1825–45); then became that college's president, a position he held for ten critical years in the life of the school from 1845 to 1854; and after the presidency remained professor emeritus in geology until his death in 1864.[2] Emily's mother, Orra White, the daughter of one of the founders of Amherst College, was a woman of many talents, particularly drawing and painting, and was in addition a fine scholar in such disciplines as Latin, Greek, and higher mathematics. She was a principal illustrator of

The Holyoke Range in the vicinity of "The Notch," where Emily gathered the orchid that became the subject for her first painting from nature. As seen from Amherst College, Massachusetts, ca. 1855. (Courtesy of the Jones Library, Inc., Amherst, Massachusetts.)

her husband's technical writings, provided drawings for his lectures, and, as a skilled botanist and artist, has left, among other works, a collection of watercolor paintings of the flowering plants and grasses of the Deerfield area of Massachusetts. An unsigned sketchbook of 120 paintings of fungi is also attributed to her.[3]

Only a few details about Emily's childhood can be found. We suspect that she had little in common in those early years with her sister Mary, who was fourteen years older than she, or even with her brother Edward, who was ten years older. Perhaps her brother Charles, only two years older, was her closest companion. We do know this, however: she was not idle. Orra Hitchcock, in a letter to her brother in Ottumwa, Iowa, dated 26 October 1846, described Emily this way: "Emily, the youngest, is nearly eight—she is very active in her habits and has an inquisitive turn of mind—a pretty good scholar for her age. She is the only daughter who has blue eyes—does not resemble *our* father's family at all."[4]

We know, too, that Emily was soon to try her hand at painting from nature. Among her flower paintings is one labeled "*Aplectrum hyemale,* Nutt. My first painting from nature. Done in Amherst 1850. From 'The Notch,' Mt. Holyoke." Emily was then twelve years old. Another painting, without a date, shows the Fringed Gentian and Cardinal Flower and bears the inscription "Painted in Amherst (when only a child)." Emily was following in her mother's footsteps: Orra White had begun her paintings of flowers at the early age of eleven.[5]

Emily's mother instructed her in drawing and painting, but she credits her father with having taught her botany.[6] Her mother was an accomplished botanist also, however, and had been a teacher of botany at Deerfield Academy as a young woman. That she studied and painted the fungi as

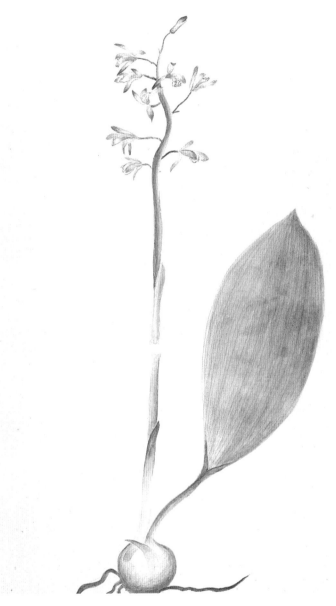

Emily Terry's first painting from nature, the orchid Aplectrum hyemale, Nutt., *done in Amherst in 1850, when she was twelve years old. She collected her specimen from "The Notch," Mt. Holyoke.*

well as flowering plants and grasses indicates more than a superficial interest in the subject. Indeed, Stephen Williams, a fellow botanist in Deerfield who knew Orra Hitchcock, referred to Emily's mother as "one of our most distinguished naturalists" and reported that "with her own hand" she had painted "with almost inimitable beauty" many of the plants her husband-to-be had collected. He continued, "She still cultivates almost all of the branches of natural history with great assiduity."[7]

With this kind of tutelage there could be little doubt that Emily would at some time in her life find fulfillment and satisfaction in the talents so well nurtured by her parents. She was ever mindful of her Hitchcock heritage. She bore the name proudly: "I can lay claim to belong to a well-known scientific family, by the name of *Hitchcock*," she wrote in the last decade of her life, and in her scientific writings and personal correspondence as well designated herself most commonly by her full name, Emily Hitchcock Terry.[8]

Emily's early formal education included attendance at lower school in Amherst and Ipswich, Massachusetts, and at Williston Seminary in Easthampton, Massachusetts, in preparation for entrance into Mount Holyoke Female Seminary. A letter from Emily's mother to Emily's brother Edward, dated 11 December 1855, mentions Emily's plans to attend Williston, where Edward was then teaching. Apparently Emily was a willing student and adjusted readily to her new environment, as her brother reports in letters to one of their sisters after a few weeks' time: "Emily is here [at Easthampton] and behaves very well—she also takes hold of study very easily and goes to bed about nine o'clock and gets up at breakfast time."[9]

Emily was a member of the class of 1859 at Mount Holyoke. Her three sisters had all preceded her at this institution; their parents were friends and supporters of Miss Lyon, the founder of the seminary.[10] We have no firsthand information about the three years Emily spent at Mount Holyoke; no letters or diaries are extant; no paintings are known from this period. Even without such sources, however, we know very well the kind of education Emily and the other members of her class were given (there were fifty-six of them). The program of study and what was expected of every student were clearly detailed in the annual catalogue.

The course at the seminary at this time was completed in three years (a fourth year was added in 1861). Candidates for admission had to pass oral examinations in English grammar, analysis of the English language, modern geography, United States history, mental and written arithmetic, algebra, Latin grammar and reading, and physiology, among other things. The three-year course included Virgil, Cicero, and Latin prose composition in each year; history, geography, botany, algebra, ecclesiastical history, chemistry, natural theology, rhetoric, literature, and more. Composition, reading, and calisthenics were required. Vocal music,

Terry's childhood study of Lobelia cardinalis, L., *Cardinal Flower, and* Gentiana crinita, Froel., *Fringed Gentian. Painted in Amherst (no date).*

penmanship, linear and perspective drawing, and French were offered, as well as instrumental music. Students were not permitted to be away from the seminary on the Sabbath. A fine program of visiting lecturers included representatives from all disciplines, such as Dr. Hitchcock himself on his favorite subject, geology. Students were expected to bring with them an English dictionary, a modern atlas, an ancient atlas, a Sabbath hymnbook, any musical works they might possess, and a commentary on the Bible. All students lived at the seminary. A public examination concluded the three-year course of study.[11]

Many years after her graduation from the seminary Emily reminisced as she wrote to her classmates: "I remember the Seminary with interest, and think especially of Miss Shattuck [instructor in botany and chemistry]."[12] It was Emily's great good fortune to come under the influence of Lydia White Shattuck, botanist-chemist-naturalist, who developed further the botanical training begun by her parents. Shattuck was an outstanding scholarly teacher who combined an aesthetic appreciation and love of plants with an absorbing interest in botany as a science. She excelled in the identification of plants, their classification, and the setting up of collections; botanical research of the day comprised all three. It is said that her students caught her energetic enthusiasm and, in the case of Emily Hitchcock at least, her inspiration was apparently enduring.[13]

The graduates of the broad, intensive liberal arts training offered at Mount Holyoke, including as it did much science as well as the basics of a classical education, were expected to become the teachers of the future. By this measure Emily Hitchcock's seminary experience was less than successful: a single session of teaching convinced Emily that it was not her métier. But as it turned out, if measured by the opportunities provided for the growth and development of one's inner resources and by the lasting influence of an inspiring teacher, her years at the seminary were ideal preparation for the days to come.

Years of Transition
1860–1870

THE MEMBERS OF THE CLASS OF 1859 OF THE MOUNT Holyoke Female Seminary called themselves the "Lulasti," an acronym formed by the first letters of the words in the class motto: "Let us live as seeing things invisible"—probably an appealing motto, it has been suggested, for students of either a scientific or a religious bent.[1] Were it not for the class letters of the Lulasti, which were published at various intervals, we would know very little of Emily Hitchcock during the years following her graduation from the seminary. These, and a few family letters, are at present our only sources of information and as such, although slim, are important and surprisingly revealing.

The first class letter of the Lulasti, dated September 1860, one year after graduation, gives us this news of Emily:

> *EMILY HITCHCOCK is "not accustomed to writing for public documents, especially, when she has nothing to say, either interesting or instructive." She has been busily occupied in being lazy (so she says,) and trying to recover her health, the former she has succeeded in doing most of the time, but the latter is not yet fully accomplished. She vis-*

its the Seminary, occasionally, and we sometimes hear of her engaged in the laudable occupation of turning those poor gentlemen's heads, over in Amherst. How many are permanently injured, we are unable to state. The class will all be happy to know that Emily's hair, after several barbaric operations, is now likely to present such an appearance at our next meeting as to fill us all with envy.[2]

Apparently Emily spent her first year after the seminary at home in Amherst and seemed content to do so.[3] Her two older unmarried sisters, Mary and Jane, were probably there as well, all doubtless giving welcome help to aging parents. Worman tells us that Edward Hitchcock was continuously sick and in pain from 1859, when he suffered a serious illness, to February 1864, when he died. Orra Hitchcock too was declining in health as she was hampered by the results of a fall in 1855 and her eyesight began to fail.[4]

The actual state of Emily's health we have no way of knowing, but whatever the problem, it was not great enough to keep her at home. Nor did it dampen her spirit of individuality if we can interpret the reference to "several barbaric operations" on her hair to mean that she had cut it off. In the 1860s short hair on a woman would have been an unusual sight.

The suspicion that Emily Hitchcock was a woman ahead of her time is given further support by the account she submitted to her classmates in the second Lulasti letter published in April 1863. She did not hesitate to make public declaration of some unorthodox opinions:

A Happy New Year to you all, dear girls, though before you can receive it, the months will have sped away, and summer will be upon us. I wish that the season of flowers might bring us all together for a Class Meeting; not one composed of a dozen or fifteen members, but including every one. As every true daughter of Holyoke should do, I have tried my fortune at teaching, and having accepted an invitation from Worcester, from August, 1861, till March, 1862, I tried my very best to enjoy it, but alas! I failed, and I then arrived at the conclusion that my duty was not in that direction; that I was not made for a disciplinarian of wilful young ladies. Unless I am sadly mistaken, I shall never again enrol myself as a school ma'am. In June, I went to visit in the family of John B. Gough, the famous orator, where I spent three months of complete happiness. I am now at home, enjoying myself in music, reading and some studying. I do not often hear from any of the class, which reminds me to say, that some of you deserve a good

*scolding. I see some of you are getting married. Well, I sup-
pose that is what we must all come to. Doleful prospect,
truly!*[5]

Clearly marriage was not at that time on Emily's list of
desiderata! Rather she reveals herself as flourishing happily
as an independent scholar: "I am . . . enjoying myself in
music, reading and some studying." It was to be the pattern
of her life. And her love of music remained with her
throughout all her days: "She was an artist with the brush,
the voice, and several instruments," it was said of her at the
end of her long life.[6] As far as we know she was successful
in adhering to her determination never again to become a
"school ma'am," but with reference to matrimony she ultimately changed her stance. The day came when she dared
to embrace that "doleful prospect."

Shortly after Emily wrote her New Year's message to
the Lulasti, events took place that dramatically altered
the course of her life. First came the death of her mother on
26 May 1863, after an illness of three months. Nine
months later, on 27 February 1864, her father died. Then
followed the breaking up of the family home. Emily's
brother Charles, writing to their brother Edward from New
York on 11 March 1864, concerning their father's death,
said, "Please extend my sympathy to Emily and Jane and
Mary—upon whom of course his loss falls more deeply
than upon any others."[7]

A strong religious faith sustained Emily during these
traumatic times:

> *Some of the most important and trying events, probably of
> my whole life, have taken place since I last wrote you. In
> May, 1863, my dear mother died after an illness of three
> months. This was my first great sorrow, and none could
> have affected me more deeply. It was a great mystery that
> my father, who so entirely depended upon her, should be
> left alone; his children tried all the more lovingly to care for
> him, but he only survived her nine months and died Febru-
> ary, 1864. Then the dear old home was broken up, and I
> can now only think of it as it was, and can never be again.
> Yet my almost bursting heart rejoices in the translation of
> my dear, sainted ones, and I am comforted in the thought
> that Heaven is my home too, and when a few more days
> have passed, our entire family circle shall be re-united
> above.*[8]

Perhaps Emily's painting sustained her as well. In this
period of stress, as in others in her life, she turned to nature
and her paintbrushes. At least we know she had not put her

painting aside, for in the winter of 1864 she sent some examples of her work to New York City where they were offered for sale. Apparently she solicited the help of her brother Edward's wife (a New Yorker by birth) with the project, who in turn sought help from her brother Lewis, a New York City resident.[9] Lewis wrote to his sister from New York on 12 February 1864: "Yours of the 6th enclosing half a dozen painted cards belonging to Emily Hitchcock came to hand during my absence in B'port [Bridgeport, Connecticut]." A week later (18 February 1864) he wrote to her again: "I have left those (5) pictures with a friend of mine Mr. C. L. Jones Bookseller on Broadway near 14th St. He will see what he can do with them. . . . We will let him sell them for what he can." He goes on to add, "Emily's ferns won't sell at all I don't believe."[10]

The flowers sold the very next day. The bookseller was right: no one cared for the ferns, as we learn from Lewis's next letter written only two days later on 20 February 1864, this time to Edward (whom he addressed as "My dear Brother"): "Mr. Jones told me yesterday that he had sold those pictures, or rather three of them (flowers). The ferns he says he can't sell. Asked him what he could allow me for them, he said twenty cents each. . . . Small enough price . . . Emily must judge if that price will pay her for her trouble." Lack of public enthusiasm for the fern paintings did not dampen Emily's own enthusiasm for this group of plants. Her early interest in the ferns stayed with her throughout her life, and she became an acknowledged authority on the ferns of Massachusetts and Vermont.[11]

In 1865, about a year and a half after her father's death and—perhaps not coincidentally—after the Civil War had ended, Emily took a bold step. She applied and was accepted at The Cooper Union in New York City to study art. "I am now taking lessons in drawing and painting in Cooper Institute," she wrote to her Mount Holyoke classmates.[12]

The Cooper Union, a coeducational, nonresidential institution located on New York's lower East Side, was founded by Peter Cooper in 1857–59 as a tuition-free college for the advancement of science and art. This unusual and forward-looking school was young when Emily attended, only in its sixth year, but its plan and purpose were established at the start by the founder and remain the same to this day. It offered a tuition-free education for promising people who wanted to learn; it practiced no discrimination of any kind—by sex, race, religion, or financial capability; and it had as its main purpose the union of science and art in an education that would enable people to lead more successful and productive lives. Part of the institution's program

Chrysanthemum Indicum.
*Done in the Pre-Raphaelite
painting class at The
Cooper Union in New York
City. Signed "E. Hitchcock
1866."*

was a school of design for women, a day school that offered "training in lead pencil and crayon drawings from casts and life, perspective and sketching from natural objects, painting in oil and water, and designing and drawing on wood, lithography, etching on stone, and painting on china." In 1865, when Emily was enrolled, Dr. William Rimmer, well-known sculptor, painter, and physician, was in charge of the School of Design; he insisted that the "ladies learn how to draw before they could paint."[13]

We can only speculate why Emily chose The Cooper Union as the place to study art, but several good reasons readily come to mind. Her training from childhood onward had been a blending of science and art as coequals: the Union was a natural extension of a concept she had long lived with. That the institution embraced a dynamic educational philosophy that was sensitive to women's needs may have appealed to this "modern" woman. That the training offered in art was good and the standards of the school were high were probably primary considerations. That students paid no tuition could well have been a deciding factor; that she had a convenient place to stay must have been important. She told her former classmates at the

Camellia Japonica, L. Done in the Pre-Raphaelite painting class at The Cooper Union in New York City. Signed "E. Hitchcock 1866." It took the first prize, Terry tells us, presumably in a student competition.

seminary: "I board at my brother's, in South Orange [New Jersey], and take the ride to and from the city [New York] every day." And her brother Charles was living in New York: "My letters should be directed to 37 Park Row, New York City, care of C. H. Hitchcock." Emily's daily commute into "the city" from northern New Jersey places her in the vanguard of those countless numbers of daily commuters between New Jersey and New York who have followed her in the 125 years since. It is safe to say that few of them were women in her day.[14]

No letters or other written records are now known to tell us what Emily thought about her art school experience or what aspects of the course she found most enjoyable or most profitable. We know only that she attended The Cooper Union in the academic year 1865–66 and fulfilled the necessary requirements to be awarded a first-class certificate, along with two other women, in the "Painting in Water Colors" course.[15] In view of the scarcity of information pertaining to her year in New York and the years immediately following, Emily's surviving paintings, each labeled with place and date, are no longer just artworks. They become in addition important biographical documents. As we turn to them for clues, we are not disappointed. Three paintings, all dated 1866 and signed "E. Hitchcock," bear the inscription, "Done [or Painted] in the Pre-Raphaelite Class at Cooper Institute in New York." One of them, an elegant study of a *Camellia Japonica* blossom, bears this additional notation: "It took the first prize."

On the basis of only slight evidence—a painting in the collection, dated 1868, done in Bethlehem, New Hampshire, and two paintings done in Amherst, Massachusetts, in 1868 and 1869—we can hazard a guess that Emily returned to New England after her year in New York. We know that in the fall of 1867 she visited the home of William Cullen Bryant in Cummington, Massachusetts; a painting in her collection is so labeled. She may well have studied nature, as she had earlier planned, and painted more during these years than these few remaining pieces would indicate, but we have no evidence to warrant even speculation.[16]

We do not need to speculate, however, about what the next major event was in the life of Emily Hitchcock. On 18 May 1870, she married the Reverend Cassius Marcellus Terry. Emily was in her thirty-second year when she married Terry, well into spinsterhood by nineteenth-century standards; Terry was not quite twenty-five years old. We can safely conjecture that their meeting was somehow connected with Amherst College, where Terry was a student and Emily's brother Edward was a professor.[17]

Terry was born in Clymer, Chautauqua County, New York, on 21 July 1845. After early schooling in Westfield, New York, he entered Amherst College in 1863. His original intention was to study law; this he abandoned when he was converted during his freshman year, and he decided to enter the ministry. He graduated with honors in 1867, ranking high as a writer and speaker. Three years later, in 1870, he graduated from Union Theological Seminary, the same spring in which he and Emily were married. In the spring of 1872 they moved to Minnesota.

The Minnesota Years
1872–1884

LESS PRIMARY DOCUMENTATION IS AVAILABLE FOR Emily Terry's Minnesota years than for any other period of her life. Her name is virtually nonexistent in Minnesota archival materials. Beyond her recognition as a plant collector by Upham in his *Catalogue of the Flora of Minnesota* (1884), the only mention we can find of her throughout the nine years of her married life spent in the state is when she is identified as the wife of Cassius Terry in his obituaries. We could rightfully expect that somewhere we would find letters. Surely Emily must have written many letters to her family in the East recounting her life and experiences in Minnesota. It is hard to believe that a woman who was such a prolific letter writer in the last decades of her life—more than one hundred of her later letters are preserved in the Archives of the Gray Herbarium Library—would not have done so. Whether not written or not preserved, unfortunately no Emily Terry letters from Minnesota are known.

Three sources of information allow us to re-create the course of Emily Terry's life in Minnesota: the obituary of her husband published in the *Minutes* of the General Congregational Association of Minnesota (1881); the documentation of her plant collections in the state as recorded by Upham in his catalogue of Minnesota's flora; and the portfolio of her paintings of Minnesota flowers that she took with her when she returned to New England after her husband's death.

We have already discovered the value of Emily Terry's paintings as biographical indicators, beyond their primary value as historical illustrations of the Minnesota flora. In addition, her Minnesota plant collections enable us to piece together, at least partially, something of her botanical activities. But for the general facts about Emily Hitchcock Terry's sojourn in Minnesota, we can only extrapolate from the information we have about her husband. Fortunately for our purposes, the Reverend Terry's Minnesota years are well documented in the unusually detailed obituary mentioned earlier.[1]

The Career of Cassius Terry

Cassius Terry's first call was to a pastorate in New Bedford, Massachusetts.[2] His plan to begin work in the Congregational church there immediately after his graduation and marriage in the spring of 1870 had to be abandoned when he was stricken with a severe hemorrhage of the lungs. He and Emily went instead to the New Hampshire hills, where several weeks of horseback riding and recuperation seemed to bring back Terry's strength and restore him to health. By the fall of 1870 he was able to take up his pastoral work in New Bedford as planned. But it was a short-lived recovery. The dampness of the Atlantic coast winter was detrimental, and Cassius Terry fell ill once more.

In an effort to find an environment in which he could regain his health, during the summer of 1871 Terry made a trip to Minnesota, where the dry, invigorating atmosphere was reported to be helpful for tuberculosis sufferers. There is no record that Emily accompanied her husband on this reconnaissance mission. While in Minnesota he visited the Indian Agencies and preached in Plymouth Church, St. Paul, then housed on Goodrich Street in a small chapel. This struggling church of only sixty to sixty-five members was on the verge of closing its doors, but the young preacher so filled them with enthusiasm that they determined to try to secure him as their pastor, in spite of his illness, of which they were well aware.[3] He would consider a call, he said, if they would consider building a new church—"no respectable man would consent to preach in such a house," he said of their present building. Terry's forthrightness must have been as appeal-

Cassius M. Terry, shown with Cardigan, one of General George Armstrong Custer's staghounds (ca. 1880). The dog was presented to Terry after the general's death at the Battle of the Little Bighorn on 25 June 1876, by his widow, Elizabeth Bacon Custer. She referred to Terry as "my husband's friend."

ing as his preaching, for the congregation did in fact start planning a new edifice and formally called him to the pastorate on 11 February 1872. After another debilitating winter on the East Coast, he accepted the call a month later. And so the Terrys, Cassius in the early stages of tuberculosis, and Emily with a new baby to care for (Edward Sweet, born 25 January 1872) as well as an ailing husband, took up residence in St. Paul in June 1872. The cornerstone of the new Plymouth Church, at the corner of Summit Avenue and Wabasha Street, was laid at the end of June.[4]

Only a few weeks later, on 19 July 1872, the Terrys' infant son died. "The death of their little boy ... was a terrible blow," the records state, and so "broken from grief at the loss" was the young pastor, and so physically weakened by the activities of the previous weeks, that the congregation granted him a vacation until fall to try somehow to throw off his sorrow and the disease that continued to plague him.

For five years Plymouth Church flourished under Pastor Terry's leadership. The new church was completed; membership increased—over two hundred new names were added to the church rolls; successful missionary and temperance societies were formed; and additional Sunday schools were started in outlying areas. He organized "one of the brightest literary societies of young people ever meeting in St. Paul." All this was accomplished in spite of

Terry's continually failing health. After a few months' or even a few weeks' work his energy was spent, and he had to seek respite and recovery in northern Minnesota, Florida, or Colorado. He would rally, only to return and find his strength quickly dissipated.

A trip to Colorado Springs in the spring of 1877 was of little help.[5] In the fall of that year Terry resigned his pastorate in Plymouth Church—a sorrowful occasion, it is reported—and went to St. Augustine, Florida. There he ministered to a Presbyterian church over the winter. But his health continued to fail. In May 1878 the Terrys returned to Minnesota and took up residence in Minneapolis, where Terry was temporarily in charge of the First Congregational Church during the regular pastor's leave in Europe.

Terry then changed his occupation entirely. For the next two years he was affiliated with the Geological and Natural History Survey of Minnesota, an organization under the jurisdiction of the Board of Regents of the University of Minnesota.[6] Of all the places Terry visited in his efforts to halt the deterioration of his lungs, apparently he had found northern Minnesota most helpful. Work with the survey took him there; it placed him in an outdoor environment, which he cared for deeply; and he could be profitably occupied while seeking recovery from his illness. We are told that " 'camping out' seemed always to restore him. Passionately fond of fishing, after the exposure and weariness of one day, sound sleep would fit him for another full day." During the summer of 1879 he was a member of the survey field party exploring the natural history of northern Minnesota, and during the winter following he worked in the laboratory, preparing microscopic sections and labeling and arranging specimens for the survey's growing natural history museum. The summer and autumn of 1880 found him back in the field studying the hydrology and distribution of forest trees in the lake region of north-central Minnesota and later compiling information on the water resources of the entire state. His account of his observations was his last productive piece of work and was included in the state geologist's report for the year 1880.[7]

As Terry's health worsened in the early winter of 1881, he and Emily set forth for Florida. He planned to return later in the summer to the notes and maps and unfinished manuscript he left behind. But a month's stay in St. Augustine in March was of no avail. It seemed best to return to Minnesota. The homeward journey had to be interrupted with a two-month stop in Aiken, South Carolina. Finally the Terrys arrived home in Minneapolis early in June. On

8 July Terry suffered the first of a series of severe hemorrhages, from which he never rallied. He died on 18 August 1881 at age thirty-six. A simple monument marks his burial place, next to that of his infant son, in Oakland Cemetery, St. Paul, Minnesota.

Several tributes to Cassius Terry indicate clearly that his early death was felt as a real loss by those with whom he had been associated. "Mr. Terry, whose promise of usefulness was very unusual . . . ," wrote one; "Dear Mr. Terry! so eloquent, so beloved . . . ," said another; and the daily newspaper spoke of his "burning words of eloquence," elaborating further, "his grand impassioned sermons will never be forgotten by those who heard them. A trained scholar, a brilliant thinker, and gifted with rhetorical powers of a rare order Mr. Terry would have unquestionably taken rank with the great preachers of this country had his physical strength been equal to his mental powers." His parishioners eulogized: "[He fought] a heroic struggle, only to die among us, but to be an inspiration to his church and leave a benediction on us all."[8] Most revealing, however, is the evaluation of Terry's contribution to the work of the Geological and Natural History Survey of Minnesota by N. H. Winchell, director of the survey:

> His [Terry's] contribution to the last report of progress, pertaining to the Hydrology of the State, shows the carefulness and the scope of his work. His perseverance and industry were remarkable, and the amount he accomplished, with his feeble health, was a surprise to those who knew the obstacles under which he labored. . . . I cannot forbear at this place, giving testimony to his uniformly cheerful disposition and urbane personal bearing, his high integrity, his zeal and industry, and his truly scientific methods of work and thought. Having spent some years in the christian ministry, one of the most instructive facts of his brief labors for the survey, is the ease and quickness with which he turned himself to purely scientific pursuits. He began with careful laboratory work, requiring patient mechanical manipulation, and he succeeded from the outset. Whatever he undertook, he knew how to accomplish at once. Having a trained mind, it was no task for him to apply it vigorously and persistently in a new field of labor. A general suggestion, or an intimation as to the direction to be given to his labor, was all that was necessary. Had he been able to finish the work that he had in hand, one of the most useful, thorough and instructive chapters of the final report of the survey would have been written by him.[9]

Three brief, but telling, comments by Emily Terry are known concerning the eleven years of her marriage, nine of which were spent in Minnesota. About midway through this period—in 1876—she wrote to her Mount Holyoke classmates: "My time is fully occupied with incessant demands upon my strength. My husband's health obliges him to go South occasionally, and this adds much to my other causes of anxiety." What those "other causes of anxiety" were we can only postulate. Obviously these were stressful years. Perhaps the tributes to her husband explain in part why, in her next message to her classmates after her husband's death, she could say: "I have had my share of sorrow, but I have been greatly blessed"; and many years later to a colleague who erroneously addressed her as "Miss," she could write, "As I was a married woman during eleven happy years, I should like to lay claim to being *Mrs.*"[10]

Emily Hitchcock Terry, Botanist and Artist

Emily Terry's life in Minnesota was complex and, we suspect, fraught with distraction and frustration, as she coped with those "incessant demands upon my strength" that she spoke of to her former classmates. It was a difficult beginning in 1872: a long train trip west with an infant and an ill husband; adjustment to a new land, a new home, a new church; the death of their son not long after their arrival in St. Paul; the never-ending worry about her husband's health.

Although Emily Terry's part in the work of Plymouth Church is not mentioned in the available church histories, we can safely assume that she was called upon to fill the traditional role of the pastor's wife by participating in the women's societies, the Sunday school, the missionary work, and, given her talents, the musical program of the church.

Particularly disruptive must have been the frequent moves in town and the travels out of town that were characteristic of the Terrys' life in Minnesota. The couple appeared to have no permanent residence; they moved several times within town as well as from St. Paul to Minneapolis.[11] The out-of-town travels, north, south, and west, dictated by Cassius Terry's illness, began almost immediately after their arrival in St. Paul and established a lifestyle that prevailed throughout their married life. Every period of work required a period of rest and recuperation; when the newly gathered strength was dissipated on more work, another respite was needed. It was a continual seeking of energy from outdoor rest and recreation, which would lead, they hoped, to Terry's complete recovery.[12]

One wonders that there was time for botany and painting in this fractionated and stressful life. Perhaps these very qualities of everyday existence made Emily's escape with her collecting case and paintbrushes as essential for her spiritual health as the outdoor life was for her husband's physical health. We know Emily accompanied her husband on his periodic necessary rest cures to northern Minnesota and elsewhere. Her plant collections in Minnesota act as mileposts along the way. The new environment must have provided absorbing and exciting botanizing, and the undisturbed time for painting must have been as welcome to Emily as camping out and fishing in Minnesota's lakes were to her husband. Despite the threat of deteriorating health that always hung over the couple, these interludes in Minnesota's wild areas, allowing each to pursue his or her own dearest passions, must have contributed much to Emily's remembrance of her Minnesota years as happy ones. And from them remain some early plant-distribution records for the state and what we believe to be the first paintings from nature of Minnesota's flora.

Collecting Minnesota's Plants

In 1884 Warren Upham's *Catalogue of the Flora of Minnesota* was published as part of the previous year's progress report of the state's Geological and Natural History Survey. The author compiled into a single list all the plants then known to be found in Minnesota: "It [the catalogue] includes not only the observations of the state geologist and his assistants upon this survey, but also those of earlier botanic collectors and explorers, enumerating all the species that are known to have been found in Minnesota by all observers up to the present time." This ambitious project, with its promise of completeness, concludes with the statement: "The total number of plants, including both species and varieties, enumerated in this catalogue and appendix, is 1650, belonging to 557 genera, and representing 118 families or orders."[13]

In acknowledging the numerous sources from which his information on the flora of Minnesota has been gathered—the first explorers, government expeditions and surveys, pioneering naturalists—Upham writes that "very important contributions of notes and specimens have been received from botanists throughout the state." In addition, he acknowledges the help of many collectors from whom

A lakeside road in Douglas County, near Alexandria, Minnesota, ca. 1895. Terry was an active collector in Alexandria and around the lakes and in the outlying areas of Douglas County. (Audio-Visual Collection, Minnesota Historical Society, St. Paul, Minnesota.)

he has received manuscript lists, "to which references are frequently made in stating the geographic range of species or localities of rare or local plants." Here we find the name of Mrs. E. H. Terry of St. Paul.[14]

After the Civil War increasing numbers of women joined the ranks of devoted amateurs who by their collecting added much to our knowledge of the natural history of the country. Minnesota had its share. Emily Terry was only one of many women who furnished data for Upham's catalogue. She was, however, one of his most active women contributors. Only Sara Manning, who collected in the Lake Pepin area, and Ellen Cathcart, collecting principally in the St. Croix, Taylors Falls, and Duluth areas, are cited more frequently by Upham than she.[15] What the sum total of Emily Terry's plant collections was we cannot say, but we do know that for more than sixty species Upham was able to use her collections as markers of geographic distribution, extension of range, or rare occurrence.[16]

It comes as no surprise that over half of the Terry records are for species found in the north-central lake area of the state. Douglas County and Alexandria, an ideal area for finding the rest and recreation required by her husband's poor health, are most frequently mentioned. *Habenaria leucophaea* (Rein or Fringed Orchis) extends "north at least to Alexandria (Mrs. Terry)," Upham notes; and *Campanula Americana* (Tall or American Bellflower), "extending north to Douglas County." She reported *Lactuca pulchella* (Blue Lettuce) at Lake Carlos, Douglas County, and *Eriocaulon septangulare* (Pipewort) from

Lake Agnes, Alexandria; the latter is noted as "rare" in the location.[17] Terry's collections defined the northern limits of several species. A tribute to her skill as a botanist is her identification of ten species of Aster (all from Douglas County), not a simple genus to work with in the large family of composites. Terry's collections are recorded for

A network of railroads, already established in Minnesota in 1873 (heavy black lines), enabled Emily Terry to collect plants at many sites (solid circles), some as far as 200 miles from the state's main urban area. (Adapted by Kristine A. Kirkeby from a map in the collection of the Minnesota Historical Society, St. Paul, Minnesota.)

other areas also, in Wright and Kandiyohi counties and in the vicinity of Winona. Her record of *Chimaphila maculata* (Spotted Wintergreen) from Clearwater in Wright County documents another rare occurrence. All these collection sites—the most distant was about 200 miles from Minneapolis–St. Paul—were accessible by railroad, which by the end of the 1870s had become the main means of travel in Minnesota. Horse-drawn vehicles were available at stations for further travel to neighboring towns not on the railroad and to yet more remote areas.

Emily Terry's botanizing was not confined to her trips into outlying areas of Minnesota. She made time for collecting while at home, at sites within and bordering the

Twin Cities: around St. Paul and Ramsey County and in Minneapolis around Lakes Calhoun and Harriet. She found *Hibiscus militaris* (Halberd-leaved Rose Mallow) on the "banks of the Mississippi River between St. Paul and Mendota"; *Streptopus amplexifolius* (Twisted-stalk) on the "bluffs near (south of) St. Paul"; *Lilium superbum* (Turk's-cap Lily) at "Excelsior, Hennepin County"; *Pontederia cordata* (Pickerel-weed) in Lake Minnetonka; and *Gentiana quinquefolia* var. *occidentalis* (Gentian) at White Bear Lake.

Although Terry made a sizable herbarium of pressed specimens during the latter years of her life in New England, we have no evidence that she did so while in Minnesota. At least, no herbarium sheets are now known, nor does Upham mention receiving specimens from her.

We have reason to believe that Emily Terry continued her interest in the flora of Minnesota even after her final return to New England in 1884. There, twenty-five years after leaving Minnesota, she had among her botanical reference works the two studies by MacMillan on Minnesota's plant life published by the Geological and Natural History Survey of Minnesota in the 1890s, several years after she had left the state permanently. There is no evidence that she ever returned to Minnesota. She continued botanizing in New England, however, where she discovered new plants, established new stations for rare plants, and ultimately became known as an authority on the ferns of the area.[18]

Bluffs along the Mississippi River below St. Paul, Minnesota, ca. 1905. Upham attributes several plant collections from this area to Terry. (E. A. Bromley Collection, Audio-Visual Collection, Minnesota Historical Society, St. Paul, Minnesota.)

Painting America's Flowers

In 1913 Emily Terry, called an "artist with the brush,"presented her bound volume of 142 watercolor flower paintings to the Department of Botany of Smith College in Northampton, Massachusetts. At the time of her death, eight years later, the collection was described as "a remarkable series of paintings of wild flowers made by her in early life."[19] On the hand-lettered title page Terry calls her work simply *American Flowers*, and below the title designates, "painted by Mrs. Emily Hitchcock Terry." Her further identification of herself is noteworthy: she points out, first and foremost, that she is the "Daughter of Professor Edward Hitchcock of Amherst College," a proud reminder that the scientist and botanist Edward Hitchcock was her mentor.[20]

As Terry aligns herself primarily with her scientist father rather than her talented artist mother—"My mother had a great deal of artistic ability," she wrote[21]—she appears to make the statement that she considers her work sound botanical illustration as well as art. Wilfrid Blunt, in his definitive study *The Art of Botanical Illustration*, has this to say about the problem of choice between science and art that faces the botanical artist:

> *The botanical artist finds himself at once and always in a dilemma: is he the servant of Science, or of Art? There can, I think, be no doubt that he must learn to serve both*

masters. The greatest flower painters have been those . . .
who have understood plants scientifically, but who have
yet seen and described them with the eye and the hand of
the artist.

And as a basic requirement for success, he adds without equivocation, "The great botanical artist must have a passion for flowers."[22]

One can question whether the dilemma postulated by Blunt (with European artists in mind) was as keenly felt by Terry and the early American botanical artists as by their European counterparts. Ella Milbank Foshay, in her comprehensive treatise on American flower painting and the botanical sciences, states: "The close connection between science and art in America has a long history. It was as early as the Colonial period, in fact, that an essential link between the scientific and artistic interpretation of nature was established." Contrary to European approaches to botanical art, which historically included floral motives in accessory roles and as decorative embellishments and evolved out of religious or still-life traditions, in America the earliest flower drawings had their origin in science and sought to be "true to nature" in order to document the flora of the New World.[23] Rather than acting in conflict the documentation and interpretation of science and art acted in concert. In fact, one of America's earliest scientific journals, the *American Journal of Science*, in its first issue in 1818 proclaimed itself dedicated to the joint documentation of natural science and art. By training, inclination, and capability Terry had learned to serve both masters from the start and was well qualified for the role of botanical artist. If the choice between science and art was a dilemma for her, no evidence of the struggle remains in her work.

The lettering throughout Terry's volume of botanical paintings from nature is all done in the same hand and is uniform in style, including the title page, species identifications, location and time of execution, and the occasional personal explanatory note. We can safely conclude that Terry herself assembled the book; there is no reason to believe that anyone other than she provided any of the information it contains.

Botanically Terry may have followed her father's lead, but artistically and in assembling her paintings into a book she followed closely in her mother's footsteps. Almost a hundred years earlier (1817, 1818) Orra White had painted the flowers and grasses growing in and around Deerfield, Massachusetts; she too painted from nature; her husband-to-be, Edward Hitchcock, had collected and named the specimens. Similarly, she had gathered her paintings into a volume, to which she gave the descriptive and intriguing title *Herbarium parvum, pictum*, a small herbarium of painted (rather than the usual pressed) specimens. Terry treasured the book highly. "It is *more* than worth its weight in gold to me," she wrote. "As I was the chief botanist among the children, she—my Mother—gave the book to me."[24]

Her mother's title, clearly indicating scientific intent, would have been appropriate for Terry's work as well. Indeed, in writing to a fellow botanist, Terry referred to her paintings in these very terms: "I would like to show you my own painted herbarium—consisting of paintings I have made from flowers, since I was a young girl. It has been gathered into a handsome book."[25] But she chose instead the title *American Flowers*, thus pinpointing the major difference between the *herbaria picta* of the two women. Orra White recorded the flora of a single region (doubtless some of the earliest illustrations of New England plants), whereas the work of the much-traveled Emily Terry is broader in scope, illustrating examples of the flora of seven states in several regions of America.[26]

About two-thirds of the paintings in the Terry collection (ninety-three) belong to her Minnesota period (1872–84). Forty-nine of these are studies of the Minnesota flora; the remainder were done primarily in Florida, Colorado, and South Carolina, while the Terrys were Minnesota residents but traveled to these states for Cassius Terry's health.[27] All except two of the Minnesota images were done between 1875 and 1878. About two-thirds of the rest of the collection (thirty-one paintings) date from 1850 to 1870 before Terry came to Minnesota; the smallest number (seventeen) were done in her post-Minnesota years, when she was engrossed in making a more conventional herbarium of pressed, rather than painted, specimens. In general, any single painting portrays only a single species; most of the exceptions, in which groups of species are depicted, are found among the paintings of the Minnesota flora. As a result, sixty-one species of Minnesota plants (plus a few that are unidentified) are illustrated in the forty-nine Minnesota paintings. Rarely did Terry add animal species to her paintings. Only three works are so embellished: one with a dragonfly; one with a dragonfly and a spider ("An aerial visitor, and an example of protective coloring in the spider," Terry notes); and one with four butterflies. Fourteen of the paintings are signed; seven signatures include the date.[28]

Mention has already been made of three paintings in the collection that remain from Terry's art-student days at

The Cooper Union. These fine, detailed studies of a chrysanthemum, a camellia, and a spray of apple flower buds were done in the Pre-Raphaelite painting class; all are signed "E. Hitchcock 1866."[29] An additional note about the camellia painting states that it took first prize, presumably in a student exhibit. The apple blossoms were no doubt an assigned subject. Foshay points out the great popularity of the apple among pomologists and orchardists of mid-nineteenth century America, a popularity that invaded the art studio. For one botanical artist at least, Martin Johnson Heade, the apple blossom was an important subject for a whole section of his oeuvre at this time (1865–70), and his many images of the apple blossom were much admired. As we see, the popularity of the subject overflowed into the classroom as well.[30]

Exposure to the Pre-Raphaelite philosophy of painting was a fortunate experience for Terry, stressing as it did the importance of realism and truth to nature, and doubtless had a major influence on her work. The Pre-Raphaelite Brotherhood, formed in 1848 by the young English painters Dante Gabriel Rossetti, William Holman Hunt, and John Everett Millais, was dedicated to correcting what the founders considered the sham standards of contemporary British painting. They aimed to recapture the honesty and simplicity that existed in Italian painting before the sixteenth century. The proponents of the movement "believed that the artist must observe a scrupulous fidelity to nature. If he painted an outdoor scene he should use the bright colors of the real countryside, and render every leaf with botanical accuracy." They believed that art should serve truth. The Pre-Raphaelite Brotherhood lasted only six years, but is considered one of the most remarkable movements in the annals of art for the effect it had on rejuvenating Victorian art.[31] That the young Cooper Union offered a course embracing the concepts of such a new revolutionary movement reflects the institution's freedom of thought and its sensitivity to the contemporary art scene—not surprising, perhaps, if we bear in mind the school's forward-looking founder.

The training in observation of detail required by the Pre-Raphaelite concepts reinforced Terry's natural sense of botanical accuracy and became an integral part of her style. Nowhere is this more evident than in her painting done in 1868 entitled "Growing on a piece of decayed wood." Terry's log with its many attendant and interrelated thriving species is a sensitive portrayal of a biological microcosm, carefully executed and faithful in its details. Such a work, depicting the flora as an integrated whole in a natural setting, can rightly be included in

"From the Bud to the Fruit." Apple flower buds, painted in the Pre-Raphaelite class at The Cooper Union, New York City. Signed "E. Hitchcock 1866."

Apple fruit, painted at the home of William Cullen Bryant in Cummington, Massachusetts, 1867.

the genre termed "ecological illustration" by Morton in his *History of Botanical Science.*[32] As Terry painted this plant community in miniature, not the usual subject for the time, she may well have been aware of the emerging scientific views of the day that perceived plants and animals not as static objects but as growing, continually

"Growing on a piece of de-cayed wood." Bethlehem, New Hampshire. Signed "E. H. 1868."

changing, and evolving organisms. Foshay discusses in detail the impact of these new scientific ideas on the character of American botanical illustration.

Most of the sixty-one species of Minnesota plants Terry illustrated are wildflowers and sedges and grasses (two are shrubs, three are trees, and four are cultivated species). The composites, sedges, and grasses are well represented, as are the Orchidaceae; twenty additional plant families are represented by one or more species.

The orchids seemed to have a special appeal for Terry: her first painting from nature (1850) was an orchid, *Aplectrum hyemale,* Nutt., and another of the three early paintings in the collection (1854) is the orchid *Pogonia verticillata,* Nutt. Among the Orchidaceae she painted during her Minnesota period, but not in Minnesota, was *Pogonia divaricata,* R. Br., which she observed in Florida with particular botanical significance, as she notes: "This painting was sent to Mr. Oakes Ames who considered it of sufficient value to extend the range to Florida, where it was painted in 1875."[33] Terry's studies of eight species of Minnesota orchids include three renditions of *Cypripedium hirsutum,* Mill. (now known as *C. reginae*), the Showy Lady's Slipper. These are at present the earliest known illustrations done from nature in Minnesota of the species that was later to become the Minnesota state flower.

That the orchids are fairly well represented in Terry's collection of paintings is to be expected; it would in fact be remarkable if they were not. Terry lived at the very time when an extraordinary "orchidomania" was sweeping out of England and Europe and engulfing the world of plant lovers. The mid-nineteenth century saw the golden age of the plant hunters, one of whom, the Czech Benedict Roezl, for example, is reported to have sent home a consignment of orchids from Central America that actually weighed eight tons! And whereas only twenty-seven orchids were described in Curtis's *Botanical Magazine* from its founding in 1787 to 1825, in a similar length of time in the mid-1800s some two hundred plates of orchid illustrations appeared in the magazine.[34]

In America the fascination with the native lady's slippers and other orchids, so strong among Victorian wildflower enthusiasts—"a certain fascination attends the very name of orchid," wrote Mrs. Dana[35]—and still prevailing today (with sometimes unfortunate results), began very early among botanists and nature lovers. Foshay says that in America from 1850 on "the orchid flower was the object of significant attention as a botanical specimen, as a popular horticultural variety, and as a design element."[36] But long before this date, in the days of John and William Bartram, two of America's earliest naturalists, the American cypripediums had already charmed English gardeners. Peter Collinson, an English botanist, in 1760 and 1761 reported the flowering of the Showy Lady's Slipper and exclaimed over the beauty that the "yellow slipper" added to his garden at Mill Hill, Middlesex, England, in May— "the yellow slipper is now in glorious flower"—plants for which he had the Bartrams to thank.[37] A hundred years before Terry illustrated the Showy Lady's Slipper in Minnesota, and before her mother had illustrated it in New England, William Bartram had painted the species in Philadelphia and sent the painting to his friend Collinson in England.

We would like to know more precisely where in Minnesota Terry collected the plants she illustrated in her paintings. Unfortunately, she gives this information for only three species. She found *Pentstemon grandiflorus*, Nutt., Beard Tongue, on the campus of the University of Minnesota; the painting of the Ram's-head Moccasin Flower (*Cypripedium arietinum*, R. Br.) was done in Clearwater, Minnesota; and her study of the Blue Violet (*Viola cucullata*, Ait.) is marked "Lake Park, Sept. 18, 1880."[38] We can speculate, but with only moderate success, about a few other locations by looking for possible connections between the species in the paintings and the notes on Terry's wildflower collections in Upham's catalogue of the flora of the state. For example, perhaps her Rein Orchis (*Habenaria leucophaea*, Nutt.) was the specimen she reported from the Alexandria area. Likewise, the *Allium stellatum*, Ker. specimen of her painting may well have been from the Alexandria area also, where Upham indicates she collected that species. This kind of speculation can be extended to only a few other paintings to which Upham's notes might apply: *Cypripedium candidum*, Muhl. may have been from near Lake Harriet, Minneapolis; *Gentiana quinquefolia*, L., from St. Paul or White Bear Lake; *Pogonia ophioglossoides*, Ker., from St. Paul; and *Hibiscus militaris*, Cav., along the banks of the Mississippi River. But for the majority of her paintings of the Minnesota flora our theories about where Terry found the specimens she illustrated must be based simply on what is known about the ranges of the species at the time and on what we know about where she botanized.

Early Botanical Art in Minnesota

During the fifty years before Emily Terry left her home in Massachusetts and headed westward in the 1870s, many people had already observed, collected, listed, and described the plants of the area we now know as the state of Minnesota. Who were these people? Did any of them illustrate their botanical finds? Or can we conclude that Terry, although far removed in time from Minnesota's first plant collectors, was nevertheless Minnesota's first botanical artist? Are her paintings the earliest illustrations of Minnesota's flora? As far as we know, this indeed appears to be so.

Apart from the early explorers, such as Father Louis Hennepin, Jonathan Carver, and Zebulon Pike, who made general note of the vegetation around them, the first natural history collectors in Minnesota were members of government-sponsored expeditions.[39] Their charge was to examine the principal geographic features of the Northwest and to prepare maps of the landforms and waterways—in other words, to describe this area of the continent. Plants were part of that great *terra incognita*. Two of the earliest of these expeditions were under the command of General Lewis Cass, governor of Michigan Territory, who during the summer of 1820 explored the Great Lakes and the upper waters of the Mississippi River; and Major Stephen H. Long, who in 1817 and 1823 explored the St. Peter's River (now the Minnesota) and the Red River of the North. Professor D. B. Douglass of West Point, botanist for the Cass expedition, collected plants, as did Thomas B. Say, the naturalist on Long's 1823 expedition. Douglass's collections resulted in the first published list of plants found in Minnesota;[40] Say's efforts, because of various misfortunes, were less successful. Similarly, an expedition led by Henry R. Schoolcraft in 1832, to determine among other things the true source of the Mississippi River, explored the central area of the state. Dr. Douglass Houghton, surgeon to the expedition, collected plants and found several new species. Yet another early explorer in the area between the Mississippi and Missouri rivers was the French scientist Joseph N. Nicollet, whose German botanist on his expeditions in 1838 and 1839, Charles A. Geyer, kept detailed notes in his botanical journal and made extensive plant collections. Sadly, the 1838 specimens were lost in transit and never found.[41] Most of the species in Geyer's catalogue were collected in Dakota Territory rather than in Minnesota. Another early collector of some importance was C. C. Parry, who in 1848 prepared a list of over seven hundred plant species in connection with a geological survey of the Northwest. Again, not all of these were Minnesota species.

As far as present research reveals, none of the reports of these explorations included illustrations. According to Michael Heinz, who is currently researching the available archival materials bearing on botanical exploration and plant collection in Minnesota from 1830 onward, the original notebooks and papers of the collectors in the 1830–51 period, where known, contain no illustrative material beyond an occasional sketch of plant parts to aid in species identification.[42] A major effort to summarize all previously listed plant species found in Minnesota as well as those in his own collections was the work of Dr. I. A. Lapham, prepared in 1865, but not published until 1875 by the Minnesota State Horticultural Society. Lapham's list includes the collections of many workers in addition to those mentioned here. The article is not illustrated, nor does Lapham mention any illustrations accompanying earlier accounts.[43]

As we hunt for botanical art in this brief survey of pre-1870 contributors to our knowledge of the flora of Minnesota, mention should be made of the federal government's Pacific railroad survey of the 1850s. The purpose of the survey, which originated in Minnesota and extended to the Pacific coast, was to determine the most practicable and economical route for a railroad. The survey's voluminous reports contain some handsome illustrations of the flora and fauna in the southern and Pacific coast areas. There are no illustrations of the flora of Minnesota.[44] Nor can we overlook the possibility that some notable artists who visited Minnesota in this period—Henry Lewis, George Catlin, Seth Eastman—may have painted the flora of the state. As far as we can determine, however, they did not. Although general views of the surrounding vegetation are part of Lewis's Mississippi River landscapes and also

Catlin's and Eastman's Indian studies, these works are in no sense botanical documentation and do not concern us here.[45]

Two equally notable, if not even more renowned, artists ventured into the vast wild country of the Upper Midwest at this time to record the native peoples, the landscape, the birds, the plants, and the animals of the North American interior. They were Karl Bodmer, the twenty-three-year-old Swiss artist who accompanied the naturalist Prince Maximilian von Wied-Neuwied (in the 1830s) and John James Audubon (in the 1840s). Their travels, in both cases on the Mississippi–Missouri waterway through the Dakotas to the edge of Montana, did not bring them into Minnesota Territory.

Another painter who traveled in the United States was Marianne North, an English botanical artist who painted spectacular plants in their native habitats all over the world. Her paintings are housed at the Royal Botanic Gardens at Kew. North crossed the continent from coast to coast in 1871 and again in 1881, but did not come to Minnesota.

One may question that botanical art found its first expression in Minnesota as late as 1875 when the plants of the area had been collected and identified as early as the 1820s. In eastern America the earliest describers of the natural history of the continent—John White, John Banister, and Mark Catesby—all left illustrations of their observations from the sixteenth to the early eighteenth centuries; William Bartram of Philadelphia, our first native-born natural history artist, produced some beautiful plant portraits in the mid-1700s;[46] Orra White (Hitchcock) made her painted herbarium of the flora of the Deerfield, Massachusetts, area in 1817 and 1818; and in 1831 Jane Kilby Welsh published her botany book in Boston, illustrated with four hand-colored plates of flowers and assorted floral and plant parts.[47] In spite of this early beginning Foshay states that in America "flower painting as a separate genre was not widely practiced until the mid-nineteenth century."[48] We must bear in mind as well that 1875 is not "late" on the scale of Minnesota's history, but is in fact quite early: the University of Minnesota was chartered in 1851 when Minnesota was still a territory; only in 1858 did Minnesota become a state; the Geological and Natural History Survey of Minnesota was established by the legislature in 1872; and the Minnesota Academy of Natural Sciences held its first meeting and published its first *Bulletin* in 1873.

Just as Terry's paintings have remained unnoticed for a hundred years and are only now being recognized, so continued research may very well bring some other work to light that will require us to revise our present beliefs. Until then, we can conclude with some confidence that Emily Hitchcock Terry was Minnesota's first botanical artist and her paintings represent the first portrayal from nature of Minnesota's flora.

A Career for the Future Emerges

From Minneapolis, Minnesota, on 19 May 1884 Emily Terry wrote to her Mount Holyoke classmates on the occasion of their twenty-fifth anniversary: "Sorrow and disappointment have placed their cold hands on our courage, but then faith comes to our aid; we rise up and go on again."[49] Three years had passed since the death of her husband. Clues are few to the events in her life during that time, but they reveal enough to allow us to construct a fairly probable scenario.

Doubtless Terry left Minnesota soon after her husband's death. She returned to Massachusetts, where she had family and roots, most probably to Amherst; her brother Edward was professor of hygiene and physical education at Amherst College. There is some indication that she served as secretary to President Seelye at the college around this time. Although this report cannot be verified, she may well have held this position briefly sometime between late 1881 and early 1883.[50]

As she reported to her classmates, in 1884 Emily Terry was back in Minnesota. The answer to why she returned to Minneapolis is found in the Minneapolis City Directory for the year 1884–85. There she is listed as the superintendent of an organization called the Woman's Industrial Exchange. The exchange, whose full title was The Woman's Industrial Exchange of Minneapolis, was founded to provide self-help opportunities for needy women by making available a market outlet for their crafts and food products. As far as can be determined, the exchange was a new effort in 1884. Terry was apparently its first superintendent; she could have been one of its founders. We might even surmise that the exchange was a project she had discussed with friends and church associates in earlier years during the planning stages, and she was persuaded to return to Minnesota to help launch its realization.[51]

Two paintings in the Terry collection, signed "E. H. Terry" and dated "'83," encourage more biographical speculation. One painting was done in Orange, New Jersey, the other in Painesville, Ohio. Terry had lived with family members in New Jersey when she was a student at

The Cooper Union in New York. Perhaps she was paying her relatives in New Jersey a springtime visit when she painted *Cornus florida,* L., a species of dogwood that blossoms in May and June. Did she then leave for Minnesota, spending some time with friends or relatives in Ohio along the way? Her painting of the fall-blooming (August-September) Trumpet Flower (*Tecoma radicans,* L.) done in Ohio suggests this as at least a possibility.

The little that we know about Terry's life in the years immediately following her husband's death understandably suggests a period of restlessness and indecision, some wandering, perhaps seeking a satisfying niche—on the whole, a time of adjustment. Involved though she was with her work for the Woman's Exchange in the spring of 1884, Terry reveals no long-range commitment to the task as she continues her letter to her classmates: "If you have any word to send me, my brother, Professor Edward Hitchcock, of Amherst, will give you my address. I am liable to change, having no permanent home, and letters are apt to go astray."

What influences next came into play we have no way of knowing. We only know that in the fall of 1884, Emily Terry, at the age of forty-six, began a new career as lady-in-charge, or head, of Hubbard House, a student residence at Smith College in Northampton, Massachusetts. She held the position for twenty-five years. Here she found her first permanent home since the death of her parents and the subsequent breakup of the family homestead in 1864. And here in New England, where she lived the remainder of her life, her interest in botany came to full fruition. Now art gave way to science in Terry's life. Briefly for her, but enduringly for us, the two were joined in her paintings of the flora of Minnesota.

Epilogue

In spite of all my troubles and worries about my ferns, I love them, and I love my work. . . . As long as I live I shall work in botany, if I have any eyes to see.

—*Emily Terry to Walter Deane (1916)*

 A FEW YEARS AFTER EMILY TERRY GRADUATED FROM Mount Holyoke Female Seminary she reported to her former classmates that she was studying art at Cooper Institute and intended to study nature afterward.[1] She no doubt was thinking ahead only a year or two when she spoke of her plans, but her statement takes on a certain prophetic quality when we consider her life as a whole. For four decades art prevailed; the study of nature came afterward. During her second forty years nothing came so close to Terry's heart as botany. This sequence may well have been the result of circumstance rather than a matter of choice. Perhaps the tools of the artist's trade were better adapted to her difficult, unsettled, and frequently disrupted younger years than was the equipment needed by the plant collector, and the ease of housing and transporting the end product in each case would have demanded consideration. Whatever the reasons, whether by choice or circumstance, the second half of Terry's life allowed botanical pursuits that found no place in her earlier years. With her return to Massachusetts, Terry seemed to start anew. The vasculum

*Emily Hitchcock Terry,
ca. 1885. Having returned
to New England after the
death of her husband,
Terry embarks upon a
new life. (Photograph by
Notman Photographic Co.,
3 Park Street, Boston,
Massachusetts. Smith
College Archives, Smith
College.)*

and press of the plant collector replaced the pad and paint-brushes and paintbox of the artist; an herbarium of pressed specimens replaced the painted herbarium; science replaced art.

For the next twenty-five years (1884–1909) Emily Terry was lady-in-charge at Hubbard House at Smith College. As administrative officer of the residence, she was responsible for its smooth functioning and for all matters that would ensure a satisfactory living experience for the young women housed there. In the Victorian 1880s and 1890s students were expected to observe house rules and rules of accept-able behavior, not to mention study hours and "lights-out" requirements, all of which had to be enforced when nec-essary. "It is late, and I must follow my 'children' upstairs, and see if their lights are out, which means that it is bed-time for me!"[2] The "matron" or "house mother" acted *in loco parentis.* She of course must be on hand to greet guests and preside at social functions. "There will be guests the whole time here [Commencement]," Terry wrote to her col-lege classmates to explain why she could spare only a few hours for her own fiftieth anniversary reunion at Mount Holyoke College.[3] All of her efforts were directed toward the well-being and general happiness of her charges. How well suited Terry was to these tasks is reflected in the following remarks made at the time of her death concerning her years of service in Hubbard House:

> *She threw into her work all the zest of her great personality. She was an artist both with the brush, the voice and several instruments. She loved music and inspired those around her with desire for good music. She was a true gentlewoman of the old school. Only those who knew her can appreciate the great place which she filled in the world, the influence which she left upon the college.*

Terry's influence extended beyond the campus and into the community, we are told, and continued to be felt after her retirement for the remaining years of her life.[4]

If there was any flaw in Terry's life at Hubbard House, it was lack of time for botany. In her letters to George Davenport, a fellow botanist and fern enthusiast, Terry often expressed regret at the large amount of time required by her "duties," by which she meant her responsibilities to the college, and the little time left for her "work," that is, her botanical studies. "I get so little time for scientific work, during the college year, that I am sometimes quite discouraged," she wrote. "I look forward to the summer months, when I have nothing else to do." The following year the problem remained the same: "This winter has been a disappointment to me, because I have not been able to give any time at all to work on ferns. I hoped to experiment with spores, even to attempting some hybridizing, but I simply have not had an hour that I could give to it. I might as well give up all thought of doing anything except my summer study and collection, and I *want* to do so much." When spring came, she was encouraged: "It looks now as if the time was at hand when one can go off to the woods and hills for ferns, and the fever is already in my blood! I can hardly wait for July when I am really free."[5]

Terry made the best resolution she could between her daily responsibilities and her inner yearnings. During the winter she organized her summer plant collections, developed her herbarium, and worked on difficult identifications, as time permitted. She grew ferns in the college greenhouse, and on at least one occasion, when she had more free time, expanded her indoor gardening with apparent success to include a challenging assortment of plants:

> *I am amusing myself by raising plants from seeds. I have some California Poppies quite well started—a good crop of dandelions, orange, grapefruit and apples. I expect to see*

grapes and pears. I have a Nemesia, which is growing—has had a profusion of beautiful golden yellow blossoms, and is now ripening seeds. It is very beautiful in the greenhouse, with all the varied colors, and the Schizanthus [Butterfly-Flower] is very beautiful.[6]

Free hours for reading in the winter months gave Terry the opportunity to keep up with events in the botanical world. Through her memberships in several societies—the American Fern Society, the Vermont Botanical Club, the Torrey Botanical Club, the American Association for the Advancement of Science, and the National Geographic Society—the new botanical literature came to her attention.[7] She followed the societies' bulletins and journals. *Rhodora,* the journal of the New England Botanical Club, was part of her regular reading: "I have taken that paper from the very beginning of its existence and value it most highly." Should a periodical be late, she lamented its delay and the inefficiency of the editor. Nor was she tolerant of a poor publishing job; she said of a new book, "I have discovered about fifty errors," all of which she considered inexcusable. She was eager for the newest information: "Tell me how I can get hold of a copy of the new Vermont Flora"; and, "Shall we ever get the new Gray's Manual? I hope to see it before I die!" (She did see it: the new seventh edition was published in 1908.) Subjects of mutual interest—collections, plant identifications, new information, new books, field trips—Terry discussed in an active correspondence with other botanists, both professional and amateur. She was equally at home with both, having been reared among the former but working among the latter as part of the strong nineteenth-century amateur tradition that contributed so importantly to American botany.[8]

As winter wore on, Terry eagerly looked forward to the special botanical joys that spring would bring. One of these was her fern garden. Although her college duties were particularly demanding during the spring semester, Terry nevertheless made time to maintain a flower bed in front of Hubbard House and a small fern garden, in which she took special delight. Many of the ferns were sent to her by her friend George Davenport: "My sincere thanks for the precious things [fern plants] which came to me yesterday from you. . . . Our gardener . . . has potted them . . . so they will be ready to put into the ground in the spring. I am very greatly pleased with them all, and hope for great results when summer comes again." The following spring she could report that the ferns had been set out in a special bed and, without exception, were flourishing. This fern garden was a repeated and continual pleasure of spring; a year later she sent Davenport a picture of "the rare ferns you sent me, every one of which is growing finely." So "precious" were these ferns that, upon her retirement two years later, Terry carefully passed on the plants, "some of the rarest of American ferns," to Harold Goddard Rugg, a fern enthusiast and one of her frequent collecting companions.[9]

Spring brought, too, the opportunity to get out in the field once again. Terry found time for plant collecting in Northampton in the vicinity of the college. She often had

Emily Terry in her flower garden in front of Hubbard House, Smith College, ca. 1905–9. (Courtesy of Arthur W. Gilbert.)

the companionship of the Reverend George H. Gilbert, whose son, Arthur, as a small child in the first decade of the 1900s, recalls seeing them on their botanical outings: "Mrs. Terry was a frequent and welcome visitor. She and my father . . . often botanized in the woods along the Mill River, she carrying the large tin specimen case with shoulder strap which I remember distinctly." The Gilbert property of three to four acres extended to the banks of the Mill River in Northampton, a beautifully wooded area "when the chestnut was still in the forest."[10]

Terry was rewarded with particular botanical success on at least two such occasions. In brief published notes she reported her discovery of two species new to Massachusetts. While exploring the woods in connection with a project aimed at making a complete list of the conifers growing without cultivation in the vicinity of Northampton, Terry

A vasculum, or botany collecting case (about eighteen inches long by seven inches wide by three inches thick), used to carry specimens while in the field, was an essential piece of equipment for the plant collector. Made of lightweight tin and fitted with a strap, it was slung over the shoulder, thus leaving hands free for steadying on a precarious path or a steep climb, as well as for gathering more specimens.

came upon a small colony of the tall form of the Common Juniper (*Juniperus communis,* var. *erecta,* Pursh.). Its longer and less crowded leaves, much greater size, and erect growth distinguished it from the usual low Common Juniper. It was the first report of the species in the state. On another spring excursion in the same area she found a sizable colony of Golden Lungwort (*Hieracium murorum,* L.) with many bright yellow blossoms, growing in a damp mossy hollow. In *Gray's New Manual of Botany* (1908) Terry's report is cited as the authority for the occurrence of the species in Massachusetts.[11]

It was the summer season, however, that brought Terry freedom and her greatest happiness in botany. For two to three months each summer she left city life and the heat of Northampton and boarded in various small communities in Maine, New Hampshire, and Vermont, all the while enjoying the luxury of botanizing at will.[12] She climbed the mountains (Dorset Mountain, at 3,804 feet, was "quite a tramp," she said—she was the first woman to reach its summit); hiked through the fields and bogs (a four-mile trek for a specimen was not too far); collected plants, especially the ferns, which were her foremost love; and prepared and pressed her collections for her continually expanding herbarium. Above all, she had the company of fellow botanists and collectors, who knew her as an accomplished and most enthusiastic botanist who was not daunted by even dangerous places. With them she could share the excitement of new finds or the discovery of a rare species or the finding of old "friends" in new locations. "My ferns are my friends, and I rejoice in everything that helps me to know them better," she said.[13]

Discovery of a plant new to an area not only attested to the botanist-collector's skill and diligence, but also brought recognition and a sense of satisfaction in having enhanced the basic knowledge of the flora. In addition to her new finds in Massachusetts, on three occasions Terry had the pleasure of making discoveries new to Vermont. She wrote to her friend and fellow botanist, Walter Deane: "[I shall] send a specimen of *Salvia verticillata* [Lilac Sage] which I found in Dorset, and which had never been found in the State before. It has persisted for some years, and I hope may be permanent. I also found *Campanula glomerata* [Bellflower]—new to the State." Her third new find was *Rhinanthus Crista-galli* (Rattle box). She continued: "The *Rhinanthus* is a seaside plant, but I found a half acre meadow that was yellow with it, in some parts of the meadow—and it seems to increase year by year. It is in Bennington, just in the newer part of the town. If there were any active botanists there, it would certainly have been found before, but it was left to me to enjoy the honor of finding it."[14] Terry did not say where or when she found the *Campanula,* but her discoveries of the other two species are well documented. In an unpublished, signed, typewritten article, preserved in the archives of the Pringle Herbarium at the University of Vermont, Terry tells of her discovery of the *Rhinanthus* on 23 June in Bennington and her finding of the *Salvia* "about the first of October following" in Dorset.[15] Although the typescript is undated, we know the year to be 1910. Terry made a painting of *Rhinanthus,* on the back of which she noted, "Found in Vermont for the first time in June 1910 at Bennington. By E. H. Terry." In her post-Minnesota life of over thirty-five years, Terry added only seventeen paintings to her painted herbarium— seven were done in Northampton, the remainder in Dorset and Bennington, Vermont. The *Rhinanthus* painting was her last addition to the collection.

Terry's intensive plant collecting, which began soon after her return to Massachusetts in 1884, quite naturally resulted in the assembling of a conventional herbarium. Through her own efforts, by exchange with other collectors, and possibly even by purchase, a not unusual practice, by 1900 her herbarium contained about 1,600 specimens of flowering plants and ferns. Day, in her survey of the herbaria of New England in 1901, described Terry's collection: "The most important part is the collection of ferns, which represents all the species, with one exception, which are described in Gray's Manual, also many of more recent discovery. In addition Mrs. Terry has specimens of ferns from western and southern United States, the West Indies, Bermuda, Labrador, Iceland, Japan, India and the Hawaiian Islands."[16] Undoubtedly Terry added many more specimens to her herbarium in the following fifteen or more years, when her most active collecting and concentrated study of ferns took place. Upon her death her herbarium of flowering plants went to Smith College; she presented her fern herbarium to Harold G. Rugg. Since Terry had collected ferns intensively in Vermont for many summers, Rugg in turn gave Terry's fern herbarium of 297 sheets to the University of Vermont as a memorial to her.[17] Examples of Terry's mounted specimens are still preserved in the herbaria of both these institutions.

Of all the places where Terry spent the summer months, none came closer to her heart than Dorset, a lovely village nestled among the hills and mountains of Vermont. It was her first choice of a place to live when she retired from her duties at the college. "I am trying to get a settled home for the rest of my life in Dorset, Vt," she wrote to the Mount Holyoke alumnae.[18] For reasons we do not know, her hopes were not fulfilled; she continued to live in Northampton until her death twelve years later. Terry knew Dorset well after many summers of plant collecting there. The area offered a great variety of ecological niches and harbored an enticing variety of flora. Not only did she have sympathetic botanists and collectors among her friends in the village, but she also had discovered Dorset to be a fern lover's paradise. Ferns of all kinds grew there—a great many of them, and in great abundance. The place drew her back like a magnet. She summered in other areas as well, but returned to Dorset again and again. She wrote: "I believe this state [Vermont] is generally conceded to be one of the most profitable for students of Ferns. Certainly Dorset is both profitable and interesting." And later: "One is never at the end, so far as ferns are concerned, in a place so favorable for their growth as Dorset. . . . Dorset is in a green valley, with mountains and high hills surrounding it. There are streams, bogs, old pastures, and deep, cold woods, where ferns delight to grow." In Dorset Terry's years of fern collecting culminated in one of her most significant botanical contributions, the complete documentation of the ferns of Dorset and vicinity.[19]

Dorset offered Terry many attractions—ferns, friends, botanists, natural beauty. We suspect the ferns were the most appealing ingredient in this winning mixture: she found more ferns in and around Dorset than in any other

Dorset Village, Vermont, in 1901, looking east from the "lookout" on Reservoir Hill. (Courtesy Dorset Historical Society.)

place she had explored. A certain rivalry is said to have existed among the fern collectors of different areas, and Terry's first published note on the ferns of Dorset in 1898 probably had more than a little to do with stimulating the competition—perhaps even beginning it.

> *At my boarding place I was known as the woman who found ferns, and requests were made to me to bring them in for general inspection. In response, one day, I said I would go for a walk, and in two hours I would bring home more than thirty varieties. Accordingly I started out to fulfill my promise, and at the time specified, I was on hand with thirty-seven varieties.*

She proceeded to list all her finds, noting that most of them grew in great abundance, even the rarities. She added further: "Indeed, the luxuriance of these two ferns [*Asplenium angustifolium* and *Aspidium Goldianum*] . . . exceeds anything I have ever seen elsewhere"; and concluded with an undisguised air of challenge: "Now in view of this long list of ferns, may not Dorset claim the first rank in point of variety?"[20]

How the fern rivalry was ultimately resolved, we will probably never know. We do know, however, that Terry was not content with her primary list of thirty-seven varieties of Dorset ferns. For several years she continued her search for species she knew must be present since the area provided the habitats suitable for their growth, if only they could be located. She sought out likely places—the limestone ledges in the mountains and spots where the rocks remained wet. Her diligence was rewarded. For example, on the ledges of Mount Aeolus, about halfway to the summit, she found a rare form of *Asplenium,* just one of the sixteen additional Dorset species she reported in the *Fern Bulletin* in 1905.[21]

The pursuit was ongoing. Two years later, during a very hot and humid summer, Terry wrote to George Davenport: "I am simply good for nothing this summer. It is quite a trial to me to give up all tramping and fern hunting, but I have not been able to go out at all. If the weather turns cool and bracing I shall try it." As fall approached and the weather improved, she was able to go out on two days. Each trip provided a new addition to her Dorset list. These, too, she reported in the *Fern Bulletin:* "It is a curious fact that one may go to the same spot, year after year, in search of the same fern and yet fail, year after year, to find it. But my persistence has been rewarded in this instance. My list now numbers fifty-five species and varieties from this locality."[22]

Terry's study of the ferns of Dorset is an excellent example of one of the favorite pursuits among botanists of the nineteenth and early twentieth centuries: the compilation of a "local flora," or the description of the plants, or a particular group of plants, within a defined area. It was a time of descriptive natural history; areas remained to be explored and described; species remained to be discovered or rediscovered in new places. An important part of the process was preserving the evidence (i.e., the plant collections) in herbaria, both private and institutional. Terry did all these things. As far as we know, she added no more ferns to her Dorset list for several years. But the project was not forgotten. Quite to the contrary. Nine seasons later—in 1915, her seventy-seventh year—she put the finishing touch on her work with the biggest effort of her collecting career. She collected more than two thousand specimens that summer (she found one more new species, bringing her total to fifty-six) and pressed, mounted, and labeled six complete herbarium sets of all the known species and varieties of native ferns growing in Dorset and vicinity. She called it "the finest happiest summer of my life."[23]

We would know little, if anything, about this final phase of Terry's study of Dorset's ferns were it not for the letters she wrote to Walter Deane, which are housed in the archives of the Library of the Gray Herbarium at Harvard University. Deane, a teacher and natural scientist who lived in Cambridge, Massachusetts, was an expert botanist and well versed in the ferns. He served as a consulting botanist and adviser to the Gray Herbarium for over thirty years and carried on a voluminous correspondence. And he saved things. The seventy-four letters from Emily Terry, mostly written between 1914 and 1916, are among over thirty-five hundred letters Deane received from close to five hundred correspondents, almost all botanists. At first the Terry–Deane letters concerned subjects of general botanical interest, but after Terry's summer of concentrated fern collecting in Dorset, they dealt almost exclusively with the Dorset ferns: double-checking identifications; exchange of specimens; and the mounting, labeling, assembly, and distribution of the herbarium sets. The enthusiastic and expert help Deane willingly offered led to a warm and deep friendship between Terry and both Mr. and Mrs. Deane, a relationship that was one of the great pleasures of Terry's final years. Terry's letters to Deane—sometimes two in a week—provide an ongoing account of the progress of the project and the difficulties she encountered along the way. Ultimately all problems were resolved, and the ambitious undertaking came to a successful conclusion. In addition, the letters contain the only record we have of the final disposition of the specimens, information only now brought to light.

By early spring of 1915 Terry had laid definite plans for the coming summer in Dorset, despite the physical handicaps that were overtaking her with the passage of time. "Some of the infirmities of advancing age are very trying!" she said. Failing eyesight was a real threat to her botanical work. A year earlier she had confessed to Deane her inability to see well enough to identify a plant new to her and appealed to him for help:

> *I do not want you to think so poorly of me as a botanist as my failure to determine these plants would indicate, for really it is my misfortune rather than my fault. If I could only study the plants as I have always done, up to three years ago, I should have fewer favors to ask. While I can always recognize my old friends among the plants, I fear I can never study out the new ones—at least when they require a lens for determination. But I have had a good time with botany all my life, and I must not complain now. . . . I can read or write all I wish, but cannot use a lens, or a needle!*[24]

Nevertheless, the advent of spring brought anticipation and enthusiasm, as it always did, and Terry revealed her hopes for the coming season to her closest botanical friends. To Dr. Merritt L. Fernald she wrote:

> *I expect to spend the summer in Dorset Vt. which is in a fine botanical region, as you know. . . . I am so much better this year, that I feel quite enthusiastic over the prospect of being able to do something in the line of my favorite science. I have made, in years past, quite an exhaustive study of the ferns of that region, and I hope to be able to make two or three complete sets of them.*

On that same day she wrote to Walter Deane, with even greater confidence: "I mean, if I have the strength and the eyesight which I *expect* to have, to make three or four collections of the native ferns of Dorset. If I am successful, I shall let you be a sharer of my joy in collecting them."[25]

As planned, Terry spent the summer of 1915 in intensive fern hunting. Besides her collecting case she carried a light portable press into the field, so she could press immediately those plants whose delicate fronds would not survive a long day in her tin vasculum. The weather sometimes hampered her work, and she was disappointed in the quality of some of her specimens. "I beg of you to be lenient to my work," she wrote to Fernald. "I was very much handicapped by the

Epilogue

Emily Terry's fern herbarium sheets of her Dorset, Vermont, collections in 1915. From the Smith College Herbarium, Smith College, Northampton, Massachusetts, where Terry deposited one of her complete sets of Dorset's ferns.

Maidenhair Spleenwort
(Asplenium Trichomanes *L.*)

Maidenhair
(Adiantum pedatum *L.*)

Ebony Spleenwort
(Asplenium platyneuron
[L.] Oakes)

Rusty Woodsia
(Woodsia Ilvensis *[L.]*
R. Br.)

great amount of rain—so that my specimens would not dry (tho I always changed the driers every day) and when they did dry, were apt to be discolored. This was very discouraging." The end result was bigger than even she had envisaged of her efforts: she pressed two thousand specimens. In the fall she sent Fernald a large packet of "all the ferns that grow in Dorset," and said: "It has been a full summer's work, and I am no longer young, but I have tramped the country over, and found every species that grows here, unless perhaps some variety or hybrid may have escaped me. . . . I have put my whole heart in it, and have worked every day—Sundays excepted—since July 4." She had little doubt about the completeness of her collection. "I feel perfectly sure that I have them all," she told Deane, and she knew them intimately: "I know every plant of *Asplenium angustifolium* in Dorset, and I 'kept tabs' on them. Not one has produced a single fertile frond this year—I wonder why?"[26]

After the summer's joy of collecting came the long and tedious work of transforming two thousand dried specimens into good herbarium mounts and assembling them into the complete fern sets Terry had promised to various people. Work on the project went on throughout the fall and into the following winter. The best specimens had to be selected for mounting; questionable identifications had to be verified (naming must be accurate beyond any question); all sheets had to be properly, correctly, and completely labeled; and finally the sheets were assembled into sets. The task might not have seemed so formidable had Terry felt well. But she was continually plagued by severe colds, the "grip," a neuralgia that sometimes prevented her walking, and, of course, poor eyesight. "I am tired. I overdrew my account in Nature's bank last summer, and have not the balance left to make it up," she explained to Deane when her progress was particularly slow.[27]

In Walter Deane, Terry found an enthusiastic helper; he had worked on numerous local floras over a thirty-year period and understood her aims. Letters between them were frequent. He solved her problems—and they were many—ably and willingly. Terry fully recognized the importance of Deane's help and was truly appreciative: "What a good man you are. I shall always say that." Finally the work was done. By the following spring Terry had completed six full sets of Dorset's ferns. She gave them to the Gray Herbarium at Harvard University; Smith College; the Vermont Botanical Club; the Dorset Society (the Dorset Science Club); Robert College in Constantinople; and, of course, to Walter Deane.[28]

Another spring came. The hard work and anxieties of the fern project dimmed in Terry's memory; her pleasure in it remained bright. Deane would understand her developing restlessness: "I feel very 'lonesome' with no ferns about in my room bothering me, and I don't half know what to do with myself!" No matter what physical difficulties she had to contend with, as spring became full blown, the fever to get out into the woods and hills was, as always, in her blood once more. A few weeks later she wrote to Deane: "I am looking forward to Dorset again, with enthusiasm but not with a *collecting* mania! tho perhaps I may find a *few* things, that will be so good I shall not care for the many. I shall not press 2000 specimens this year!" A week later her eagerness to "do more in her favorite science," as she had said in the past, was clearly with her still: "I feel as if the time was near for looking for 'more worlds to conquer' in the fern line. If I find anything of interest you will be likely to know of it, but it will not be like last summer's strenuous work. If I had good eyes I would try my hand at the grasses but oh! dear, I mustn't even think of it!" The grasses are among the most difficult of plant families for the collector and taxonomist. Emily Terry sought challenges to the end.[29]

The last years of Terry's life are represented by only a few letters in Deane's collection of Terry correspondence. On 25 November 1918 she wrote to him about a fern of some special interest she had raised with success in the Smith College fern house and her intention to send him photographs of it. "I will send them as soon as I can. I find myself quite handicapped some days, for want of sufficient energy to do anything, even as little strenuous as doing up a photograph to send you! Truly I believe it must be true that I am 80!" On 9 November Terry had celebrated her eightieth birthday. Apparently Deane remembered the day with a bouquet. "My flowers from the birthday offering are nearly gone—one or two white chrysanthemums remain."[30]

A letter written by Terry the following spring, dated 1 April 1919, is the last in Deane's collection. He had asked for a copy of her birthday picture. "How good of you to ask for this film, and to suggest an enlargement of the picture. It would be *fine*. Here it is, if you really want to do it, and of course you would not suggest it otherwise.—So here's my hearty thank you, which goes with the film." The letter is signed, "Good night for this time. E. H. T." The picture is in Deane's collection of photographs and is inscribed on the back, "Emily H. Terry. On her eightieth— 9 November-1918."[31]

Sometime in the early spring of 1920 Terry suffered a stroke that left her disabled and her mind confused. Two postcards bring Deane's Terry file to a sad close. Written by one of Terry's neighbors on South Street in Northampton,

Emily Terry celebrates her eightieth birthday. (Walter Deane Photographic Collection, Archives, Gray Herbarium Library, Harvard University, Cambridge, Massachusetts.)

they brought Deane news of her condition: "I spent the day at the hospital Thursday, and Mrs. Terry was really much about the same—certainly not any better. Yesterday her condition was if anything a trifle worse, her mind is very disturbed. . . . Dr. thinks her condition may be such for quite a time as she has a wonderful constitution. I hope however, that it will be of short duration. I read your letter to her—it came when I was there." And three weeks later: "I was up to see Mrs. T. yesterday and found her much the same, certainly *not* any better. . . . She hasn't got many callers. The Dr. did not think it best. She is always more strenuous after callers have been. . . . We all hope for the end soon but we cannot tell. I will give Mrs. T. your regards."[32]

Many years earlier, when her good friend in botany
George Edward Davenport died, Terry included some
thoughts about her own death in a letter of condolence to
Davenport's daughter. She had learned of Davenport's sudden death while he was walking in his "beloved [Middle-
sex] Fells." "I could not help thinking, What a beautiful
way to go! Sudden death is what I long and pray for—yet
I know the shock to friends is very severe. But I think a
long drawn out illness is in the end much harder to bear."
As she thought further about the loss of her friend, she
went on to express her philosophy about a life after death:
"I am glad to believe that I shall see him again. . . . My
father fully believed that he should study the stars when he
acquired a spiritual body. Why shall we not all carry on our
study of the works of our Creator, when we have passed
from earth?" In her mind the spirit of learning was eternal.[33]

Unfortunately, sudden death was not Emily Terry's fate.
She lay ill for almost a year before she died in the Dickin-
son Hospital in Northampton on 6 February 1921. She was
in her eighty-third year.

Terry left clear instructions in her will: "I wish my body
to be cremated and the ashes thrown to the winds. I desire
my name to be inscribed upon the stone in Oakland Cemetery, St. Paul, Minnesota, where my husband and child are
buried." And so it was done. Her name as she liked best to
see it—Emily Hitchcock Terry—and the date of her death
are carved there in bold letters. Above every other time and
place Emily Terry wanted to be identified with her life in
Minnesota, a brief interlude when, for her, art and nature
were joined and which, decades later, she remembered as
happy years.[34]

When Emily Terry retired from the administrative staff
of Smith College in 1909, her friends and admirers, want-
ing to pay her tribute, established a scholarship fund in her
honor. The action they took is best described in the words
of the document formulated at the time:

> *After twenty-five years honorably spent in the service of
> Smith College, Mrs. Emily Hitchcock Terry has resigned
> her post as lady in charge of the Hubbard House. . . .
> Alumnae and former members of the college who lived in
> the Hubbard House while it was under Mrs. Terry's care,
> desiring to express in a permanent form their appreciation
> of her long, faithful and efficient services, as well as their
> own affectionate regard for her, have raised a fund for that
> purpose. . . . It is the purpose and intention of the donors
> of said fund that Mrs. Terry shall enjoy the income thereof
> during her life, and that upon her death said fund shall be
> devoted to the maintenance of a permanent scholarship to*

*be known as The Emily Hitchcock Terry Memorial Schol-
arship . . . which shall be awarded annually . . . to a deserv-
ing student or students of Smith College for her or their aid
and support, in the pursuit of her or their studies at [the]
college.*[35]

The Emily Hitchcock Terry Memorial Scholarship is still
in effect and still bears her name.

Publications of Emily Hitchcock Terry

1898. "Dorset Ferns." *Fern Bulletin*, vol. 6, no. 1, pp. 7–8. (January 1898)

1900. "Another Locality for *Schizaea.*" *Fern Bulletin*, vol. 8, no. 2, p. 36. (April 1900)

1901. "*Juniperus communis*, var. *erecta*, in Massachusetts." *Rhodora*, vol. 3, no. 29, p. 146. (May 1901)

1905. "*Hieracium murorum* in Massachusetts." *Rhodora*, vol. 7, no. 76, p. 80. (April 1905)

1905. "*Dicksonia pilosiuscula* forma *schizophylla* in Vermont." *Rhodora*, vol. 7, no. 77, p. 99. (May 1905)

1905. "More about the Ferns of Dorset." *Fern Bulletin*, vol. 13, no. 3, pp. 84–85. (July 1905)

1907. "Herbarium-making of a Century Ago." Vermont Botanical Club, *Bulletin* no. 2, p. 28. (April 1907)

1907. "Additional Dorset Ferns." *Fern Bulletin*, vol. 15, no. 2, p. 49. (April 1907)

[1910.] "Two Good Finds." Unpublished manuscript, Archives of the Pringle Herbarium, Department of Botany, University of Vermont, Burlington. 2 pp.

Notes

Prologue

1. *Third Class Letter of the Lulasti [Class of 1859], Mount Holyoke Female Seminary, April, 1866* (Northampton, Mass.: Trumbull and Gere, 1866), 13. Mount Holyoke College Library/Archives, South Hadley, Mass. (Hereinafter cited Mount Holyoke College Library/Archives.)

2. Letter, Emily Hitchcock Terry to Walter Deane, 13 August 1914. Walter Deane Papers, Archives, Gray Herbarium Library, Harvard University Herbaria, Cambridge, Massachusetts. (Hereinafter cited WDP, Gray Herbarium Library.)

3. Warren Upham, *Catalogue of the Flora of Minnesota, including its Phaenogamous and Vascular Cryptogamous Plants, Indigenous, Naturalized, and Adventive.* The Geological and Natural History Survey of Minnesota, Annual Report of Progress for the year 1883, Part VI (Minneapolis, Minn.: Johnson, Smith and Harrison, 1884).

The Early Years
1838–1859

1. Emily Hitchcock's birth date is erroneously reported in several places, including notably on her death certificate, which therefore also reports her age at death incorrectly. The date used here is that recorded in the office of the town clerk, Amherst, and given by Emily on a Mount Holyoke College alumnae census card on 7 December 1914 (alumnae file of Emily Hitchcock Terry, class of 1859, Mount Holyoke College Library/Archives). This date is also recorded in Mrs. Edward Hitchcock, Sr., *The Genealogy of the Hitchcock Family Who Are Descended from Matthias Hitchcock of East Haven, Conn., and Luke Hitchcock of Wethersfield, Conn.* (Amherst, Mass.: Carpenter and Morehouse, 1894), 447. The statement that Emily was born in the president's house at Amherst College (H. G. Rugg, "[Obituary of Emily Hitchcock Terry]," *American Fern Journal* 11 [1921], 93) is likewise erroneous. Professor Hitchcock did not become the president of Amherst College until 1845. Sources of information about Emily Hitchcock are few, and, in addition, discrepancies are frequent within even this small body of data. For example, Emily stated that she was the eighth child of Edward and Orra Hitchcock (Deerfield Academy Archives, Deerfield, Massachusetts), whereas the genealogy of the Hitchcock family cited above records the following seven children born to this couple: Edward (1822), Mary (1824), Catharine (?), Edward (1828), Jane Elizabeth(1833), Charles Henry (1836), and Emily (1838).

2. Mrs. Edward Hitchcock, Sr., *The Genealogy of the Hitchcock Family*, 443–46.

3. The talents and accomplishments of Edward and Orra White Hitchcock are well discussed in the following detailed and scholarly article: Eugene C. Worman, Jr., "The Watercolors and Prints of Orra White Hitchcock," *AB Bookman's Weekly* 83 (1989), 646, 648, 650–68. Orra White's folio of paintings of flowering plants, bearing the date "1817, 18," is housed in the Deerfield Academy Archives, Deerfield, Massachusetts. The unsigned sketchbook of paintings of fungi, *Fungi, selecti picti*—dated 1821 and labeled "Said to have been painted by the mother of Mrs. Emily Hitchcock Terry," all in an unidentified hand—is held in the Smith College Archives, Northampton, Massachusetts. On the basis of handwriting and certain stylistic similarities, Worman concurs with the attribution of this work to Orra White Hitchcock. To lend strong support to the correctness of the attribution of the book of 120 watercolors of fungi to Emily's mother, we need only cite a letter written by the famous botanist John Torrey to L. D. von Schweinitz, a fellow scientist, on 3 May 1822, in which he said: "A few days ago a friend of mine (the Rev. Ed. Hitchcock of Conway, Mass.) sent me for examination a book of drawings of Fungi 120 in number, done by his wife" ("The Correspondence of Schweinitz and Torrey," *Memoirs of the Torrey Botanical Club* 16 [1921]). There can be little doubt that the book housed in the Smith College Archives is the book examined by Professor Torrey in 1822.

Although a note by an unknown person on the inside front cover of the sketchbook states that the book was given to Smith College by Mrs. Terry, actually no information is known at the present time, either in the archives at the college or elsewhere, that corroborates this statement (telephone communication, Smith and Maida Goodwin, archivist, Smith College, 22 July 1991). It should also be pointed out that no mention of paintings of fungi has been found in Emily Terry's letters or her other known writings when she discusses her mother's botanical work. She speaks only of her mother's painted herbarium. If Terry was the donor, which indeed seems highly likely, she may have made the gift to Smith College early in her affiliation with that institution, which would have preceded by many years her preserved writings.

Orra White Hitchcock's painted herbarium and sketchbook of the fungi, as well as many of her other nonbotanical artworks, were on public display for the first time in 150 years in the spring of 1991 in the Russell Art Gallery of the Reed Center for the Arts at Deerfield Academy.

4. Letter, Orra Hitchcock to her brother, 26 October 1846. President Edward Hitchcock Papers (Box I, Folder 7), Amherst College Archives. I am indebted to Eugene C. Worman, Jr., for calling to my attention the material quoted here and elsewhere from the President Edward Hitchcock Papers, and I express my gratitude to him.

5. E. C. Worman, Jr., "The Watercolors and Prints of Orra White Hitchcock," 646.

6. Margaret R. Hitchcock, "And There Were Women Too," *Amherst Graduates Quarterly* 1937, 191; Letter, Terry to Deane, 13 August 1914. WDP, Gray Herbarium Library.

7. Stephen W. Williams, "Report on the Indigenous Medical Botany of Massachusetts," *Transactions of the American Medical Association* 2 (1849), 863–69. Williams believed that flower paintings had a particular value and wrote that paintings were "the most permanent and beautiful method of preparing what may be called a fac-simile of an herbarium. There is no danger of the destruction of the paintings from insects, and of the fading of the plants from the ravages of time." More about early botany in the Deerfield area can be found in William W. Jenney, "'American Herbarium': Key to Deerfield's Historic Landscape," *Historical Journal of Massachusetts* 15 (1987), 61–69.

8. Letter, Terry to Deane, 13 August 1914. WDP, Gray Herbarium Library.

9. Notes by Anna C. Edwards, class of 1859, Mount Holyoke Female Seminary, in the alumnae file of Emily Hitchcock Terry, class of 1859. Mount Holyoke College Library/Archives; letters, Orra Hitchcock to Edward Hitchcock, 11 December 1855 (Box I, Folder 15), Edward Hitchcock to sister, 21 December 1855, 28 December 1855 (Box I, Folder 15). President Edward Hitchcock Papers, Amherst College Archives.

10. According to records in the Mount Holyoke College Library/ Archives, Mary Hitchcock attended Mount Holyoke Female Seminary for one year, 1841–42, and is considered a nongraduating member of the class of 1844; Catharine attended for two years, 1842– 43 and 1844–45, graduating in 1845; Jane attended for one year, 1851– 52, and is recorded as a nongraduating member of the class of 1854. Like Emily, Mary was interested in botany. She was listed in the botanical directory of the Torrey Botanical Club in 1873 (ferns were her speciality), and she was also a member of the Connecticut Valley Botanical Society in 1875.

11. *Twenty-Second Annual Catalogue of the Mount Holyoke Female Seminary, in South Hadley, Mass. 1858-9* (Northampton, Mass.: Bridgman and Childs, 1859). Mount Holyoke College Library/ Archives.

12. *Fifth Class Letter of the Lulasti [Class of 1859], Mount Holyoke Female Seminary, October, 1876* (Northampton, Mass.: Gazette Printing Company, 1876), 18. Mount Holyoke College Library/ Archives.

13. Charlotte Haywood, "Lydia White Shattuck," in Edward T. James et al. (eds.), *Notable American Women 1607–1950: A Biographical Dictionary* (Cambridge, Mass.: Belknap Press, Harvard University, 1971), 273–74.

Years of Transition 1860–1870

1. Patricia J. Albright, College History/Archives Librarian, Williston Memorial Library, Mount Holyoke College, South Hadley, Massachusetts.

2. *First Class Letter of the Lulasti [Class of 1859], Mount Holyoke Female Seminary, September, 1860* (Northampton, Mass.: Metcalf and Company, 1860), 15. Mount Holyoke College Library/Archives.

3. An incident that Terry recounted to Walter Deane many years later, as she reflected on her youth, could well have occurred at about this time. George Lincoln Goodale, the subject of her reminiscences, at the time of writing (1914) held the Fisher Professorship of Natural History at Harvard University (the chair vacated by the death of Asa Gray). In 1856–60 Goodale was a student at Amherst College and was assistant in the Botany Department in 1860–61. Terry wrote: "I so much wish you would take [a picture] of Professor Goodale, for I would like to see if he is now like the man I remember so well. I am delighted to hear again from him, and specially pleased that he remembers the box of 'little things,' which my friend Miss Cora Welch of New Haven and I took such juvenile delight in preparing. I shall never forget. . . . Ask him if he remembers, in connection with the 'little things' that we dubbed him 'Andropogon furcatus'? I think he named that grass for me. These reminiscences are very delightful, recalling my early days." The box of "little things" was most likely a collection of natural history objects—plants and seeds, perhaps, as well as other "collectibles." The grass referred to is commonly known as Beard Grass, characterized by bearing florets in racemes on prominently bearded stems. We can only conclude that Professor Goodale already in his youth wore the handsome beard that we see in later photographs of him. We suspect that botanical adventures such as this were frequent occurrences in Terry's life. (Letter, Terry to Deane, 25 August 1914. WDP, Gray Herbarium Library.)

4. E. C. Worman, Jr. "The Watercolors and Prints of Orra White Hitchcock," 666–67.

5. *Second Class Letter of the Lulasti [Class of 1859], Mount Holyoke Female Seminary, April, 1863* (Northampton, Mass.: Trumbull and Gere, 1863), 13. Mount Holyoke College Library/Archives. The orator referred to, John B. Gough, was born in Kent, England, in 1817, and died in West Boylston, Massachusetts, in 1886. Gough struggled with alcoholism for many years, finally succeeded in overcoming the habit, and became a well-known and highly regarded temperance lecturer. He was noted for his charismatic and persuasive performances as an orator. He lectured in the large and small towns of Massachusetts and elsewhere in the East and traveled on at least two occasions to England, where he had successful lecture tours (*National Cyclopedia of American Biography* 3 [1893], 336).

6. From remarks made in chapel service at Smith College on 7 February 1921, announcing the death of Emily Hitchcock Terry on the previous

day in Northampton. Smith College Archives, Northampton, Massachusetts. (Hereinafter cited Smith College Archives.)

7. Letter, Charles Hitchcock to Edward Hitchcock, 11 March 1864. President Edward Hitchcock Papers (Box I, Folder 24), Amherst College Archives.

8. *Third Class Letter of the Lulasti [Class of 1859], Mount Holyoke Female Seminary, April, 1866,* 13. Mount Holyoke College Library/ Archives.

9. Edward's wife was Mary Lewis Judson. At this time Edward was professor of hygiene and physical education at Amherst College. The family probably lived in Amherst, and Emily would have been in close touch with them.

10. Letters, Lewis Judson to Mary L. Judson Hitchcock, 12 February 1864, 18 February 1864. President Edward Hitchcock Papers (Box I, Folder 24), Amherst College Archives.

11. Letter, Lewis Judson to Edward Hitchcock, 20 February 1864. President Edward Hitchcock Papers (Box I, Folder 24), Amherst College Archives.

12. *Third Class Letter of the Lulasti [Class of 1859], Mount Holyoke Female Seminary, April, 1866,* 13. Mount Holyoke College Library/Archives.

13. The following two biographies of Peter Cooper are excellent sources of information about The Cooper Union: Edward C. Mack, *Peter Cooper: Citizen of New York* (New York: Duell, Sloan and Pearce, 1949); and Miriam Gurko, *The Lives and Times of Peter Cooper* (New York: Thomas Y. Crowell, 1959). Mack (pp. 269–71) tells us that when The Cooper Union opened its doors in 1859, a veritable mob appeared for registration. In all the classes about 2,000 pupils were admitted; over 600 soon dropped out. Of the 1,366 who remained, 120 were women in the School of Design (later the School of Art). By 1883 applicants to the art school had to wait an entire year to be admitted. Peter Cooper's attitude toward women, unusual for the time, bears mention. Gurko writes: "Peter [Cooper] urged that 'usefull arts' be taught, so that young ladies might, he explained, 'earn decent and respectable livings, and especially that they shall be kept from marrying bad husbands.' . . . It distressed Peter to see young girls make unwise or loveless marriages just for the sake of getting someone to support them. . . . He felt that it was especially important to provide women with the best possible training so that they might be economically independent if the need arose" (pp. 175–76).

14. Quotations from the *Third Class Letter of the Lulasti,* 13. Mount Holyoke College Library/Archives. Emily's older sister Catharine had married Henry M. Storrs, who became a pastor and served churches in several places, among them Orange, New Jersey (Mrs. E. Hitchcock, Sr., *The Genealogy of the Hitchcock Family,* 446). It was with this family that she boarded while studying in New York City. Whereas present travelers between New Jersey and New York use automobiles, buses, trains, and bridges and tunnels over and under the Hudson River, Emily's mode of travel would have been the Morris and Essex Railway from South Orange to Hoboken, New Jersey, and the Barclay St. Ferries across the river to New York.

15. *Cooper Union Annual Report* 7 (1865–66), 46. The Library, The Cooper Union, Cooper Square, New York City.

16. In "One Hundred Year Biographical Directory of Mount Holyoke College 1837–1937" (*Bulletin Series* 30 [1937], 94) the city of New Haven, Connecticut, is given as Emily Hitchcock's residence in 1868–69. At the present time no documentation is known that either supports or refutes this statement.

17. Terry and Hitchcock were married in Boston, Massachusetts, by the Reverend J. H. Seelye, later president of Amherst College (Mrs. E. Hitchcock, Sr., *The Genealogy of the Hitchcock Family,* 447). In a genealogy of Terry families published in 1887 (Stephen Terry, *Notes of Terry Families in the United States of America* (Hartford, Conn.: [Publ. by the compiler], 172), Terry's name is given as Cassius Millard. He is referred to as Charles M. in one of his obituaries. In most instances his name is given as Cassius M. or C. M. Terry. On a Mount Holyoke College alumnae

census card Emily Terry gives her husband's full name as Cassius Marcellus Terry, which is here accepted as Terry's correct name (alumnae file of Emily Hitchcock Terry, Mount Holyoke College Library/Archives).

The Minnesota Years 1872–1884

1. "In Memoriam [Cassius Marcellus Terry]," *Minutes, Appendix E* (General Congregational Association of Minnesota, 1881), 45–46. According to Anne A. Hage, historian and archivist of the Minnesota Conference, United Church of Christ, Minneapolis, Minnesota, this obituary is unusual in length and exceptional in detail for its time and attests to the high esteem in which Cassius Terry was held by his parishioners. Additional obituaries appeared in the *Minneapolis Tribune*, 19 August 1881, 6; and the *Evening Journal (Minneapolis and St. Paul)*, 19 August 1881, n. p.

2. Principal sources of information about the ministry of Cassius Terry, in addition to the obituaries already mentioned, are the following: *Plymouth Church of St. Paul, Minnesota, 1858–1898: Celebration of Its Fortieth Anniversary, June 12–19, 1898* (St. Paul, Minn.: Rich and Clymer, 1899), 8, 17–19, 34–36; Warren Upham, ed. (with others), *Congregational Work of Minnesota 1832–1920* (Minneapolis: Congregational Conference of Minnesota, 1921), 276, 396; Nelson Handsaker, *History of Plymouth Congregational Church and the Merged Park and Grace Churches, Saint Paul, Minnesota, 1858–1968* (1968), 14–16.

That the only known photograph of Cassius Terry shows him with General George A. Custer's dog Cardigan provides the opportunity to relate an incident in Cassius Terry's life that may at first glance seem arguably too removed from the subject of botany and botanical illustration in Minnesota to be included here. If justification is needed, we can state unequivocally that it presents a fine illustration of the fascinating and intriguing ancillary paths down which the researcher may unexpectedly be led in the ongoing search for truth. And we cannot overlook the very real possibility that this incident affected Emily Terry's life. I am indebted to archivist Penelope Krosch at the University of Minnesota Archives for providing me with the basic facts of the case. I learned of it while making inquiry about materials in the archives bearing on Terry's employment with the Minnesota Natural History and Geological Survey, of which, by the way, there were none. Instead, Krosch introduced me to Custer's staghound Cardigan and his relationship to Cassius Terry. I thank her for supplying me with this information as well as the photograph of Terry and other related materials.

To understand the story of Cassius Terry and Custer's dog Cardigan we need to know a few historical facts. In March 1873 General Custer and the entire Seventh Cavalry were ordered to Dakota to control the Indians and thus secure the peaceful building of the Northern Pacific Railroad. The transfer of the unit from Kentucky to Dakota was made via river steamer from Memphis and by train northward from Cairo. The party consisted of 800–900 men and as many horses, and all the equipment such a force would require: camping and household supplies and gear; military necessities; saddles and so forth for the horses—on the whole, a mammoth undertaking. The road ended in Yankton; from there on the party was "on the march" on horseback over a 500-mile stretch westward to their permanent base in Dakota Territory. Soldiers' and officers' wives were part of the huge moving column, among them, Elizabeth Custer, the general's wife, who rode at the head beside her husband. Finally the long trek was over; their new permanent base was Fort Lincoln, south of Bismarck. Mrs. Custer recounted the events of the trip and her subsequent life in Dakota in her book *Boots and Saddles; or, Life in Dakota with General Custer* (first published in 1885; reprinted by Corner House Publishers, Williamstown, Mass., in 1969).

For our purposes one of the most noteworthy ingredients of this large westward-moving military assemblage was the pack of about forty staghounds and deerhounds (not to mention new puppies, half-grown dogs, and cages of mockingbirds and canaries) that accompanied the general and Elizabeth wherever they went. The general was an ardent hunter. When the column made a halt the hounds were released and the hunt was under way. "The pack of hounds were an endless source of delight to the general," wrote Mrs. Custer. When making camp at night the dogs all followed them into their tent. She continued, "If it were very cold when I returned from the dining-tent, I found dogs under and on the camp-bed and thickly scattered over the floor. . . . If I secured a place in the bed I was fortunate." In the pack was Cardigan.

Custer took several of his favorite dogs with him on his campaigns. The first expedition to the Yellowstone took place the summer of 1873; the Black Hills expedition in the summer of 1874; and the second expedition to the Yellowstone in 1876, which ended so disastrously at the Battle of the Little Bighorn. Cardigan was with him in the Black Hills in 1874, but he was not along on the ill-fated journey to the Yellowstone in 1876—perhaps he was too old to withstand the rigors of the march. It has been said that Cardigan was the general's favorite dog, but he was in fact Elizabeth's favorite. She described him: "My favorite, a great cream-colored staghound, was named 'Cardigan.' He never gave up trying to be my lap-dog. He was enormous, and yet seemingly unconscious of his size. He kept up a perpetual struggle and scramble on his hind-legs to get his whole body up on my lap."

After Custer's death at the Little Bighorn, Elizabeth was faced with the task of disposing of the hounds. She sought the help of a Mr. C. W. McIntyre of St. Paul; what the overall result of this effort was we do not know. We do know very well, however, what happened to Cardigan. Elizabeth herself gives us this account: "I will . . . speak of the final fate of Cardigan. When I left Fort Lincoln I asked some one to look out for his welfare, and send him, as soon as possible, to a clergyman who had been my husband's friend. My request was complied with, and afterwards, when the poor old dog died, his new master honored him by having his body set up by the taxidermist, and a place was given him in one of the public buildings in Minneapolis. I cannot help thinking that he was worthy of the tribute, not only because of the testimony thus given to the friendship of the people for his master, but because he was the bravest and most faithful of animals." That the Minneapolis clergyman was Cassius Terry there can be no doubt, as the accompanying photograph here attests. The public building Elizabeth Custer refers to was the University of Minnesota's zoological museum, where Cardigan stood on view in a glass case for the next forty years.

In 1923, for reasons not now known, someone no longer identifiable appeared at the university museum looking for Cardigan. The dog was no longer there. This precipitated some concern and discussion. Dr. Thomas S. Roberts, then director of the museum, explained that two years earlier he had discarded the mount because it was not of general interest, and because of its condition it was thrown onto a pile of refuse. Cardigan's fate thereafter is unclear. Someone reported that the discarded mounted animal had been rescued from the rubbish heap by a janitor with a strong historical sense. It is said that the dog was later displayed in a small museum of sorts in downtown Minneapolis. And there the trail ends. Accounts of the investigations of the whereabouts of Cardigan, his identification as the mounted hound on public display for so many years, and the identification of Cassius Terry as his owner were all reported in the *Minneapolis Tribune* (22, 24, 25, and 27 March 1923). Had the inquirers of 1923 known of Elizabeth Custer's account of her disposition of Cardigan they would have had to look no further for answers to many of their questions.

All that remains is to find some explanation of how the friendship between George Custer the general and Cassius Terry the clergyman came about. They were not just passing aquaintances apparently; Mrs. Custer called Terry "my husband's friend." The Custers were at Fort Lincoln from 1873 to 1876, the years during which Terry was becoming well known for his work and preaching at St. Paul's Plymouth Church. During those years the Custers habitually visited New York City during the winter months. Since St. Paul was the main railroad center at the time, their trips invariably brought them through St. Paul, as did their trips to Michigan to see the general's parents. Also in St. Paul during the same years, stationed at Fort Snelling, was General Alfred C. Terry, George Custer's commander and his friend. Although Alfred Terry and Cassius Terry were in fact remotely related, we have no basis for believing that they knew each other. But it is not unlikely. Perhaps General Terry introduced the young couples to each other on some occasion when the Custers were stopping over on one of their trips. In addition, people were sometimes marooned in St. Paul because of the weather. We know of at least one such occasion in the Custers' travels: just a few months before the Battle of the Little Bighorn, George and Elizabeth Custer were delayed in St. Paul because the railroad was completely snowed in. They were in St. Paul from February to April in 1876. These facts give rise to some quite plausible explanations of how these two probably very different men became friends. Perhaps more research will yield the answer; for now we can only speculate.

One final word. We do not know just when Cardigan came to live with the Terrys; it could have been as early as July 1876. Nor do we know how long the dog lived. The best estimate of the date of the picture shown here is ca. 1880. Is it possible that Emily Terry's statement to her Mount Holyoke classmates in the fall of 1876 that her time was fully occupied with "incessant demands" on her strength was related to the introduction of an "enormous" staghound into her life? It is a legitimate question.

3. In the twentieth century it may seem strange that a person known to be ill with tuberculosis (in Terry's day called consumption) would be hired to fill a position that entailed frequent and close public contact with large numbers of people. We must remember that the infective nature of the disease was not known in the 1870s and that its mechanism of transmission was not recognized and understood until the momentous work in bacteriology by Louis Pasteur, Robert Koch, and others in the years 1880–90, the very decade in which Terry died.

4. The church was completed a year later. At the invitation of Cassius Terry, the poet John Greenleaf Whittier wrote a hymn for the dedication of Plymouth Church on 19 June 1873 (W. Upham, *Congregational Work of Minnesota 1832–1920*, 488–89).

5. Discrepancies between dates in church records, which state that this Colorado trip took place in 1877, and those on Emily Terry's Colorado Springs paintings, which are labeled 1878, make it difficult if not impossible to make definite statements about the Terrys' comings and goings in these years. It is entirely possible that dates were confused in Emily Terry's memory as she assembled her volume of paintings many years after she had done them.

6. N. H. Winchell, *The Geological and Natural History Survey of Minnesota, Eighth Annual Report for the Year 1879* [1880], 8; *Ninth Annual Report for the Year 1880* [1881], 8–9; *Tenth Annual Report for the Year 1881* [1882], 6–7. For putting me in touch with the materials of the Minnesota Geological Survey and for sharing his knowledge of the survey's early history I am grateful to Professor G. B. Morey, professor and associate director and chief geologist, Minnesota Geological Survey, University of Minnesota, St. Paul.

7. C. M. Terry, "The Hydrology of Minnesota, A Report of Progress," *The Geological and Natural History Survey of Minnesota, Ninth Annual Report for the Year 1880* (1881), 224–80.

8. Notes by Anna C. Edwards, class of 1859, Mount Holyoke College Library/Archives; *Plymouth Church of St. Paul . . . Celebration of Its Fortieth Anniversary*, 35; "Rev. C. M. Terry [Obituary]," *Minneapolis Tribune*, 6; W. Upham, *Congregational Work of Minnesota*, 271–79.

9. N. H. Winchell, "Summary Statement," *The Geological and Natural History Survey of Minnesota, Tenth Annual Report for the Year 1881* [1882], 5–8.

10. *Fifth Class Letter of the Lulasti*, 18. Mount Holyoke College Library/Archives. *Sixth Class Letter of the Lulasti [Class of 1859], Mount Holyoke Female Seminary, October, 1876, to June, 1885* (Boston, Mass.: Beacon Press, 1885), 41. Mount Holyoke College Library/Archives; Letter, Terry to Deane, 13 August 1914. WDP, Gray Herbarium Library.

11. St. Paul City Directories, 1873 through 1877–78; Minneapolis City Directories, 1878–79 through 1880–81.

12. In 1878 alone, Emily Terry painted the flora in Colorado Springs, Colorado; St. Augustine, Florida; Chautauqua County, New York; and

Minnesota (probably at several locations); and in 1879, in Massachusetts, as well as in Florida and Minnesota.

13. Warren Upham, *Catalogue of the Flora of Minnesota* (1884), 5, 182.

14. Ibid., 9, 10. It is entirely possible that Emily Terry and Warren Upham were acquainted before Upham came to Minnesota in 1879 to assist N. H. Winchell, geologist and director of the Geological and Natural History Survey of Minnesota. Upham, a native of New Hampshire, attended Dartmouth College, Hanover, New Hampshire, where he studied geology under Charles Henry Hitchcock, Emily's brother. Further, from 1874 to 1878 he assisted Hitchcock, who was state geologist of New Hampshire at the time, and also made substantial contributions to Hitchcock's work *Geology of New Hampshire* ([Biographical sketch of Warren Upham], Esther Jerabek, Minnesota Historical Society). Upham's period of affiliation with the Minnesota Survey included the years 1879–81, when Cassius Terry was also employed by the survey. The men were companions in two seasons of fieldwork during those years. Cassius Terry's service with the survey may well have been an outgrowth of Emily's connection with Upham and with the survey through her plant-collecting activities. If Emily Terry and Upham were not previously acquainted, it is not hard to imagine that Professor Hitchcock would have sent Upham off on his westward journey to Minnesota with a letter of introduction to his sister who lived there.

15. In addition to the numerous citations by Upham of collections by Sara Manning and Ellen Cathcart, two publications document the notable contributions by these women to our knowledge of the flora of Minnesota. Manning's paper, "The Wild Flowers of Lake Pepin Valley," published in the annual report of the Minnesota State Horticultural Society for the year 1884, includes a catalogue of 504 species. Cathcart's collections of thirty species and three varieties of Minnesota ferns were reported in the *Bulletin of the Minnesota Academy of Natural Sciences* for 1877 (published in 1878) by W. H. Leonard ("The Filical Flora of Minnesota").

16. As recorded in Upham (1884), Terry botanized in the following areas: St. Paul; Ramsey County; banks of the Mississippi River between St. Paul and Mendota; bluffs south of St. Paul; White Bear Lake; Mendota; Winona; Hennepin County; Minneapolis; Lake Harriet, Minneapolis; Lake Calhoun, Minneapolis; Excelsior; Lake Minnetonka; Alexandria; Douglas County; Lake Agnes, Douglas County; Lake Carlos, Douglas County; Clearwater, Wright County; Clearwater Lake, Wright County; Lake Elizabeth, Kandiyohi County; Green Lake, Kandiyohi County. Doubtless Terry collected at many other sites that did not yield unusual finds and therefore were not worthy of special note by Upham in his catalogue.

17. Terry's botanical nomenclature has been retained throughout this work. For the species illustrated in the accompanying plates the modern scientific and vernacular names are given as well.

18. Conway MacMillan, *The Metaspermae of the Minnesota Valley*, Report of the Minnesota Geological and Natural History Survey of Minnesota, Botanical Series I (Minneapolis, Minn.: Harrison & Smith, 1892); *Minnesota Plant Life*, Report of the Geological and Natural History Survey of Minnesota, Botanical Series III (St. Paul, Minn. 1899). Terry contributed several volumes, including these books, numerous texts and scientific papers by Asa Gray, and works by other botanists, from her personal library to the library of the Vermont Botanical Club in 1909 when she retired as lady-in-charge at Hubbard House, Smith College (*Vermont Botanical Club, Bulletin* 4 [1909], 7).

19. H. G. Rugg, "[Obituary of Emily Hitchcock Terry]," *American Fern Journal* 11 (1921), 93–94.

20. Terry's volume of paintings is housed in the Rare Book Room of the Smith College Library. For a number of years (1973–91) it was in the library of the Arcadia Nature Center and Wildlife Sanctuary in Easthampton, Massachusetts.

21. Mrs. E. H. Terry, "Herbarium-making of a Century Ago," *Vermont Botanical Club, Bulletin* 2 (1907), 28.

22. Wilfrid Blunt, *The Art of Botanical Illustration* (New York: Charles Scribner's Sons, 1951), 3–4.

23. Ella Milbank Foshay, *Nineteenth Century American Flower Painting and the Botanical Sciences* (Ph.D. dissertation, Columbia University, New York City, 1979), 19. (Available from University Microfilms International, Ann Arbor, Michigan.) This in-depth work is "a study of the relationship between scientific, particularly botanical, perceptions of nature and the development of the flower genre in nineteenth-century America," and the change in the representations of flowers during the century as botanical views of nature changed. It is "not a survey history of American flower painters and their works. . . . It is, instead, an examination of parallel shifts in the fundamental scientific and aesthetic views of the natural world, and their reflections in images of flowers in nature" (from the author's abstract).

24. Letter, Terry to Deane, 16 November 1914. WDP, Gray Herbarium Library. Orra White's *Herbarium parvum, pictum* is housed in the Deerfield Academy Archives, Deerfield, Massachusetts. Terry called her mother's painted herbarium "a most beautiful and interesting thing." She described the volume and its history in a small article entitled "Herbarium-making of a Century Ago," published in the *Vermont Botanical Club, Bulletin* 2 (1907), as well as in an undated note she appended to the work. Stephen W. Williams, a Deerfield physician-botanist, described the area where the plants Orra illustrated were collected in an article, "Report on the Indigenous Medical Botany of Massachusetts," published in the *Transactions of the American Medical Association* 2 (1849), 863–69.

In his study of the watercolor paintings of Orra White Hitchcock, Worman (1989) states that Orra White's painted herbarium was donated to Deerfield Academy by Mrs. Terry. This would appear to be a safe assumption. In fact, however, according to Patricia Venneri, archivist at Deerfield Academy, there is no record of any kind in the archives or elsewhere, as far as we know, that tells how, when, or from whom Deerfield came into possession of this work (telephone communication, Smith to Venneri, 22 July 1991). In the light of Emily Terry's last will and testament, it is surprising that it is at Deerfield at all. In her will, signed on 31 March 1914, Terry gave detailed directions for the disposition of her mother's volume of paintings, clearly one of Terry's most valued treasures and obviously still in her possession at the date of signing: "The Herbarium painted by my mother before her marriage I give and bequeath in trust to my nephew, John S. Hitchcock, to hold and enjoy the same for and during the term of his natural life. Upon his death I give this Herbarium to the Trustees of the Smith College, for its botanical department to be kept with my own painted Herbarium, which I have already given to said Smith College." Why Emily Terry's stated instructions miscarried and her wishes were not fulfilled is a mystery, and unless additional information comes to light, so it will undoubtedly remain. There is, of course, always the possibility, not to be overlooked, that at some later time Terry reconsidered her bequest and decided that, by its very nature, her mother's volume would be more appropriately placed at Deerfield Academy and that somehow this was done and her will was not altered to reflect the change.

25. Letter, Terry to Deane, 26 September 1914. WDP, Gray Herbarium Library.

26. Three additional states (New Hampshire, New Jersey, and Ohio) are each represented by only a single painting.

27. Although Terry has labeled fifty of her paintings as Minnesota plants, one of these clearly is a labeling error since the two species shown do not grow in Minnesota. The painting probably was done in Florida, where both species are found and where she made other paintings in the year indicated on the mislabeled work.

28. Terry signed her work in various ways: E Hitchcock, with date; E. H., with date; E. H. T.; E. H. T., with place and date; E. H. Terry; and E. H. Terry, with date.

29. When assembling the collection Terry erroneously assigned the date

1867 to the apple blossom painting; the painting itself is clearly marked 1866.

30. E. M. Foshay, *Nineteeth Century American Flower Painting,* 295 f. In the spring of 1870 Martin Heade's good friend Frederick Church wrote him a letter in which he exclaimed over the spectacular floral display in his orchard and regretted that he was unable to invite him to "come up and appleblossomate for a few days."

31. Tom Prideaux et al., *The World of Whistler, 1834–1903* (New York: Time-Life Books, 1970), 61–62, 68.

32. A. G. Morton, *History of Botanical Science* (London, New York: Academic Press, 1981), 154. Morton uses the term ecological illustration to describe Albrecht Dürer's painting *The Large Piece of Turf* (ca. 1503).

33. Dr. Oakes Ames (1874–1950), whose special interests were orchids and economic botany, was professor of botany at Harvard University, as well as director of the Harvard Botanical Museum and supervisor of the Arnold Arboretum. In the course of his study of the Orchidaceae he described more than 1,000 new orchid species. His orchid herbarium numbered more than 64,000 specimens (presented to Harvard University), and his collection of living orchids was the most complete assemblage of orchids in the United States (presented to the New York Botanical Garden). As the author of 300 publications, most of which dealt with orchids, Ames was considered one of the world's leading orchidologists (*National Cyclopedia of American Biography* 53 [1971], 569–70).

34. For more information about the colorful saga of the worldwide orchid hunters, see Tyler Whittle, *The Plant Hunters* (Philadelphia, New York, London: Chilton, 1970), 143–48. Other comments on this plant-craze phenomenon are found in E. M. Foshay, *Nineteeth Century American Flower Painting,* 299 f.; and R. G. C. Desmond, "The Botanical Magazine—Chronicle of Gardening Taste," in Ruth L. A. Stiff, *Flowers from the Royal Gardens of Kew* (Hanover and London: University Press of New England, 1988), 16–17.

35. Mrs. William Starr Dana (Parsons, Mrs. Frances Theodora [Smith] Dana), *How to Know the Wild Flowers: A Guide to the Names, Haunts, and Habits of Our Common Wild Flowers* (New York: Charles Scribner's Sons, 1896).

36. E. M. Foshay, *Nineteeth Century American Flower Painting,* 304.

37. Joseph Ewan (ed.), "William Bartram—Botanical and Zoological Drawings, 1756–1788. Reproduced from the Fothergill Album in the British Museum (Natural History)." *Memoirs of the American Philosophical Society* 74 (1968), 35.

38. Lake Park is in Becker County near Detroit Lakes, where we know Cassius Terry worked with the Minnesota Geological and Natural History Survey in the summer and fall of 1880.

39. The following references, all excellent sources of information about the early geographic and natural history explorations of Minnesota, have contributed to the material in this section: John Dobie, *The Itasca Story* (Minneapolis, Minn.: Ross and Haines, 1959); Lucile M. Kane, June D. Holmquist, and Carolyn Gilman (eds.), *The Northern Expeditions of Stephen H. Long: The Journals of 1817 and 1823 and Related Documents* (St. Paul: Minnesota Historical Society Press, 1978); Susan Delano McKelvey, *Botanical Exploration of the Trans-Mississippi West—1790–1850* (Jamaica Plain, Mass.: Arnold Arboretum, Harvard University, 1955); Warren Upham, *Catalogue of the Flora of Minnesota* (1884).

40. D. B. Douglass, "Notice of the Plants Collected by Professor D. B. Douglass, of West Point, in the Expedition under Governour Cass, during the summer of 1820, around the Great Lakes and the Upper Waters of the Mississippi: The Arrangement and Description, with Illustrative Remarks, Being Furnished by Dr. John Torrey," *American Journal of Science* 4 (1822), 56–69.

41. Edmund C. Bray and Martha Coleman Bray (trans. and eds.), *Joseph N. Nicollet on the Plains and Prairies: The Expeditions of 1838–39 with*

Journals, Letters, and Notes on the Dakota Indians (St. Paul: Minnesota Historical Society Press, 1976).

42. Unpublished data. I am most grateful to Michael Heinz, Minneapolis, Minnesota, for discussing his research with me and for permitting me to cite his work here.

43. I. A. Lapham, "A Catalogue of the Plants of Minnesota," *Transactions of the Minnesota State Horticultural Society* (1875), 89–118.

44. U.S. War Department, *Reports of Explorations and Surveys, to Ascertain the Most Practicable and Economical Route for a Railroad from the Mississippi River to the Pacific Ocean*. Made under the direction of the secretary of war, in 1853–[1856] (Washington, D. C., 1855–60, 12 volumes in 13 parts).

45. Well-illustrated accounts of the life and work of these artists are the following: Henry Lewis, *The Valley of the Mississippi Illustrated* (St. Paul: Minnesota Historical Society, 1967); Harold McCracken, *George Catlin and the Old Frontier* (New York: Dial Press, 1959); John F. McDermott, *Seth Eastman: Pictorial Historian of the Indian* (Norman: University of Oklahoma Press, 1961).

46. J. Ewan (ed.), "William Bartram—Botanical and Zoological Drawings," 4.

47. Jane Kilby Welsh, *The Pastime of Learning, with Sketches of Rural Scenes* (Boston, Mass.: Cottons and Barnard, 1831).

48. E. M. Foshay, *Nineteeth Century American Flower Painting*, 38.

49. *Sixth Class Letter of the Lulasti*, 41. Mount Holyoke College Library/Archives.

50. Emily Terry is not listed in the City Directory for either St. Paul or Minneapolis, Minnesota, in the years 1881–83. Her secretaryship to President Seelye is mentioned in the *Seventh Class Letter of the Lulasti [Class of 1859], Mount Holyoke College, South Hadley, Massachusetts, June, 1885 to July, 1899* (Holyoke, Mass.: Hubbard and Taber, 1899), 27. Mount Holyoke College Library/Archives. President Seelye, the same Rev. J. H. Seelye who had married the Terrys eleven years earlier, was president of Amherst College from 1876 to 1890. Annie L. Rutledge, archives associate at the Amherst College Library, states: "I was unable to locate any reference to her [Terry] ever holding this position [secretary to President Seelye]. This is not to say that she didn't, but that a record of her employment was not kept in the President's Office Records" (letter, Rutledge to Smith, 17 November 1989).

51. A brochure, published by the Woman's Industrial Exchange in 1886, which was located at the time at 25 Fourth Street South (Collum Block) in Minneapolis, reports on the progress of the exchange during the two and a half years of its operation, details the services offered, and describes the rules governing patrons and depositors. According to listings in the city directory, the organization was in existence for seven years. (Collections of the Minnesota Historical Society.)

Epilogue

1. *Third Class Letter of the Lulasti [Class of 1859]*, 13. Mount Holyoke College Library/Archives.

2. Letter, Emily Hitchcock Terry to George Edward Davenport, 23 March 1906. George Edward Davenport Papers, Archives, Gray Herbarium Library, Harvard University Herbaria, Cambridge, Massachusetts. (Hereinafter cited GEDP, Gray Herbarium Library.)

3. Notes by Anna C. Edwards, class of 1859, Mount Holyoke College Library/Archives.

4. Remarks made in chapel service, Smith College, 7 February 1921, announcing Terry's death. Smith College Archives; H. G. Ruff, [Obituary—Emily Hitchcock Terry] (1921).

5. Letters, Terry to Davenport, 17 March 1905; 23 March 1906; 20 May 1906. GEDP, Gray Herbarium Library. George Davenport (1833–1907), an amateur botanist who lived in Massachusetts, was a recognized authority on North American ferns. He assembled an important herbarium, published many articles, belonged to several scientific societies, and carried on an extensive correspondence with other students of

ferns, both amateur and professional, of whom Terry was one. Well over two thousand letters from botanists are housed among the George Edward Davenport Papers in the Library of the Gray Herbarium, including forty-one letters from Terry between 1904 and 1908. They deal with the collecting, identification, and exchange of ferns and are the principal source of information about Terry's botanical interests during these years. When Davenport died, Terry wrote to Merritt L. Fernald (2 February 1908, Historical Letters, Archives, Gray Herbarium Library, Harvard University Herbaria), "How sad Mr. Davenport's death—I feel a personal loss, for he has been such a kind and generous friend to me."

6. Letter, Terry to Deane, 4 April 1915. WDP, Gray Herbarium Library. In her letters Terry reveals a close personal relation with Dr. Ganong, head of the Department of Botany at Smith College during the year she was affiliated with the college. Access to the college's greenhouse facilities was a privilege she still enjoyed in her retirement years. I had the pleasure of being shown the greenhouses where Terry worked by Dr. C. John Burk, Gates Professor in the Biological Sciences at Smith College and curator of the Smith College Herbarium. These now historic houses are still in use.

7. Mount Holyoke College alumnae census card, filled out by Terry 7 December 1914. Mount Holyoke College Library/Archives. Terry joined the American Fern Society in 1893 and was elected to membership in the Torrey Botanical Club in 1902. There is no doubt that the Vermont Botanical Club, which she joined in 1903, was Terry's favorite organization; she attended the meetings even though as far removed from Northampton as Burlington, Vermont. "I *just love* that Vermont Club— they have some of the finest men and women in it that I know anything about." (Letter, Terry to Fernald, 2 February 1908. Historical Letters, Gray Herbarium Library.)

8. The only collections of Emily Terry correspondence now known are in the archives of the Library of the Gray Herbarium, Harvard University. Most of these letters were written to George Davenport and Walter Deane; others were written to Drs. Merritt L. Fernald, Benjamin L. Robinson, and Edmund W. Sinnott. From her letters we know that Terry had many other correspondents; unfortunately her letters to them are not extant as far as we know. The quotations in this paragraph are taken from the following letters: Terry to Deane, 19 August 1914, WDP; Terry to Davenport, 7 February 1906, 16 March 1906, 5 August 1906, GEDP; Terry to Fernald, 22 October 1902, Historical Letters. All in the archives of the Gray Herbarium Library.

9. All quotations from letters, Terry to Davenport, 20 October 1905; 20 May 1906; and 17 July 1907. GEDP, Gray Herbarium Library. Rugg mentioned the disposition of Terry's ferns in the Terry obituary he wrote for the *American Fern Journal* (1921). Rugg, a librarian at Dartmouth College, Hanover, New Hampshire, maintained a large fern garden at his family home in Proctorsville, Vermont.

10. Letter, Arthur W. Gilbert to Beatrice Scheer Smith, 9 January 1990, and interview 23 May 1990, in Dorset, Vermont. One of my pleasantest experiences while researching the life of Emily Terry was meeting Mr. Gilbert and visiting with him and his wife in their family homestead in Dorset. George Gilbert, his father, brought the family to this home in the early 1900s for the summers, and after 1912 they lived there permanently. Gilbert ancestors occupied the house from around 1854 onward. Emily Terry was a frequent visitor in the Gilberts' Dorset home, as she had been in their Northampton home, and she "continued her botanizing" there.

11. E. H. Terry, "*Juniperus communis,* var. *erecta,* in Massachusetts," *Rhodora* 3 (1901), 146; "*Hieracium murorum* in Massachusetts," *Rhodora* 7 (1905), 80.

12. Terry's summering places included Willard, Maine; Starrking and Wonalancet, New Hampshire; and Bennington, Dorset, Hartland, and Pittsford, Vermont. She was not equally enthusiastic about them all. Of Wonalancet, where there were no botanists, she said: "*How can* people go to a lovely country place, and not care for its flora? I do not see." Terry to Deane, 30 March 1915. WDP, Gray Herbarium Library.

13. Letter, Terry to Davenport, 8 November 1904. GEDP, Gray Herbarium Library.

14. Letter, Terry to Deane, 30 October 1914. WDP, Gray Herbarium Library.

15. E. H. Terry, "Two Good Finds." Unpublished typescript, 2 pp. Archives of the Pringle Herbarium, Department of Botany, University of Vermont, Burlington. I am indebted to Professor David S. Barrington, curator of the Pringle Herbarium, for bringing this note to my attention. I appreciate his help.

16. Mary A. Day, "The Herbaria of New England," *Rhodora* 3 (1901), 281–83.

17. *Vermont Botanical and Bird Clubs, Joint Bulletin* 9 (1923), 48.

18. Notes by Anna C. Edwards, class of 1859. Mount Holyoke College Library/Archives.

19. E. H. Terry, "Dorset Ferns," *Fern Bulletin* 6 (1898), 7–8; "More about the Ferns of Dorset," *Fern Bulletin* 13 (1905), 84–85.

20. E. H. Terry, *Fern Bulletin* 6 (1898). Arthur W. Gilbert, although he can supply no documentation concerning the fern rivalry, says that everyone at the time was aware of at least one such competition for finding the greatest number of ferns, that between Dorset and Manchester (Gilbert to Smith, in interview, Dorset, Vermont, 23 May 1990).

21. E. H. Terry, *Fern Bulletin* 13 (1905). Mount Aeolus, elevation ca. 3,230 feet, was named by Professor Charles Hitchcock, Terry's brother, in 1860. He brought his geology classes to the mountain, not only to study its geology but also to see an important bat cave there (Tyler Resch, *Dorset: In the Shadow of the Marble Mountain* [West Kennebunk, Maine: Phoenix Publishing, 1989]).

22. Letters, Terry to Davenport, 5 August 1906, 11 September 1906. GEDP, Gray Herbarium Library; E. H. Terry, "Additional Dorset Ferns," *Fern Bulletin* 15 (1907), 49.

23. Letter, Terry to Deane, [1916]. WDP, Gray Herbarium Library. The new addition to the fern list was *Asplenium simulatum* Davenp., which represented "a considerable extension of the range in Vermont of this rare fern" (*Vermont Botanical Club, Joint Bulletin* 2 [1916], 35).

24. Letters, Terry to Deane, 6 March 1916, 26 September 1914. WDP, Gray Herbarium Library.

25. Letters, Terry to Fernald, 30 March 1915. Historical Letters, Gray Herbarium Library; Terry to Deane, 30 March 1915. WDP, Gray Herbarium Library.

26. Letters, Terry to Fernald, Fall [1915]. Historical Letters, Gray Herbarium Library; Terry to Deane, 4 November 1915, 10 March 1916. WDP, Gray Herbarium Library.

27. Letter, Terry to Deane, 27 January 1916. WDP, Gray Herbarium Library.

28. Letter, Terry to Deane, 27 March 1916. WDP, Gray Herbarium Library. Terry recounted her distribution of the herbarium sets to Deane (letter, [winter 1916]): "My original plan was to send the set of ferns to Dr. Fernald [Gray Herbarium, Harvard University], Mr. Walter Deane, and Dr. Ganong for Smith. Then I added, as a matter of course, Dr. Burns, for the Vermont Botanical Club. Then Dr. Post [professor at Robert College, Constantinople] was so appealing in his very great interest, and from the fact that everything was new—as he had always lived in Constantinople, I promised him a set. After that I learned that the new society in Dorset would like contributions, so of course I promised them a set. . . . Dr. Gilbert (Pres. of the Dorset Society [Dorset Science Club].)." In the spring of 1990 I had the pleasure of seeing one of Terry's sets of ferns at the home of Arthur W. Gilbert in Dorset. Terry's obituary in the *American Fern Journal* (1921) states that a set was "preserved in the village library in Dorset." None of the Terry herbarium sheets could be found either in the Dorset Village Public Library or in the Dorset Historical Society Museum when I made inquiry in 1989, but through the persistence of Elisabeth B. Sturges, a former president of the Dorset Historical Society, Terry's collection was found in the basement of the home

of a former curator of the Historical Society, where it had been put about twenty years before for safekeeping. The specimens are in surprisingly good condition and at the present time are housed in the Dorset Village Public Library. Recently (October 1991) an additional set of about forty herbarium sheets of Terry's 1915 Dorset fern collections was discovered in the Dorset Historical Society Museum by William H. Manley, curator of the society. Whether this set exactly duplicates the first set discovered has not yet been determined.

29. Letters, Terry to Deane, 27 March 1916, 15 April 1916, and 23 April 1916. WDP, Gray Herbarium Library.

30. Letter, Terry to Deane, 25 November 1918. WDP, Gray Herbarium Library. References to other exchanges between Terry and Deane indicate that more letters were written during these years, but for some reason they were not preserved.

31. Letter, Terry to Deane, 1 April 1919. WDP, Gray Herbarium Library.

32. Postcards, B. D. Strang to Deane, 13 April and 3 May 1920. WDP, Gray Herbarium Library.

33. Letter, Terry to Miss Davenport, 9 February 1908. GEDP, Gray Herbarium Library.

34. In choosing cremation Terry proved herself once again a person of independent thought and a woman ahead of her time. According to the manager of the Springfield Cemetery in Massachusetts, where Terry's body was cremated, only 137 persons elected cremation there in 1919–21, whereas 1,200–1,300 bodies were cremated at the Springfield Cemetery in 1990.

35. Document concerning establishment of The Emily Hitchcock Terry Memorial Scholarship, 1909. Smith College Archives, Smith College.

American Flowers

PAINTED BY

MRS. EMILY HITCHCOCK TERRY

Description of the Volume

EMILY TERRY'S MOUNTED PAINTINGS, BOUND together, form a volume 18½ inches high, 14½ inches wide, and about 4 inches thick. The book has a quarter-leather binding: the boards are covered with yellow-brown bookcloth, the spine is covered with medium-brown leather. Imprinted on the spine in gold uppercase block letters is:

FLOWER / PAINTINGS / — / EMILY HITCHCOCK TERRY

Inside, the pages are pale tan-grey lightweight tagboard, 18 inches high by 13¼ inches wide, smooth glossy on the back, faced on the front with a matte-finish laid paper of the same color. The title page bears the following inscription in manuscript, centered on the page in eight lines:

American flowers.
painted by
Mrs. Emily Hitchcock Terry
Daughter of Professor Edward Hitchcock of Amherst College,
Head of the Hubbard House at Smith College, 1884–1909
and by her presented
to the Department of Botany of Smith College
June 1913.

The title page and all captions throughout the volume have been lettered in the same hand in uniform style with a fine-point pen in black ink.

The book contains 142 watercolor paintings, one of which has been laid in. Another laid-in study, unidentified and unfinished, is not included in these tabulations. Size of the paintings differs widely: height ranges from 4⅝ inches to 15½ inches, and width from 2⅝ inches to 12 inches. Paintings are done on paper of various surface textures and colors: white, off-white, cream, gray, buff, ecru, aquamarine, pale blue, robin's egg blue, blue gray, very pale green, and yellow green. All colored papers are in muted tones. Each subject is identified with a caption in manuscript, which generally gives the scientific name and the common name; date and place of execution; and occasional explanatory notes. The paintings are mounted singly, with one exception, on unnumbered pages, which are bound into the volume according to the sequence observed in *Gray's New Manual of Botany* (7th edition, 1908).

It is necessary to state again that fixity or rigidity in botanical nomenclature is unattainable, either in Latin or vernacular names although the tendency is naturally toward uniformity in practice. Species are not fixed and invariable entities. Demarcation between species and varieties is open to interpretation. Not nearly all the plants on the earth are yet discovered. Conclusions of careful investigators must be recorded. Knowledge in any science is subject always to modification and new statement, whether in physics or chemistry or biology. When knowledge and its formulas become static the science decays. There is no finality in interpretations of nature.

—*Liberty Hyde Bailey and Ethel Zoe Bailey in* Hortus Second
(New York: Macmillan, 1941).

Explanation of Plate Legends

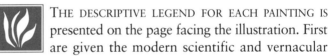 THE DESCRIPTIVE LEGEND FOR EACH PAINTING IS presented on the page facing the illustration. First are given the modern scientific and vernacular names, the nomenclature according to *Vascular Plants of Minnesota* by Gerald B. Ownbey and Thomas Morley (Minneapolis: University of Minnesota Press, 1991). Then follows Emily Terry's caption, exactly as she wrote it. Research in the intervening hundred years has clarified species' relationships, making some of her plant names obsolete (even accepted punctuation has changed: a comma is no longer used between the scientific name and the authority for it, and many specific epithets, formerly capitalized, are no longer written thus).

Complete citations for the two works referred to frequently in the plate legends are Warren Upham, *Catalogue of the Flora of Minnesota* (Minneapolis: Johnson, Smith and Harrison, 1884); and Barbara Coffin and Lee Pfannmuller, *Minnesota's Endangered Flora and Fauna* (Minneapolis: University of Minnesota Press, 1988).

The plates are arranged according to the sequence set forth in *Gray's New Manual of Botany* (7th edition, 1908), the order also observed by Terry in her book.

The Minnesota Flora
Plates 1–46

1 *Sagittaria graminea*
  Sagittaria latifolia   Duck-Potato, Wapato

2 *Bouteloua hirsuta*   Grama-Grass
  Bouteloua curtipendula   Side-Oats Grama

3 *Vulpia octoflora*   Six-Weeks Fescue
  Festuca pratensis   Meadow-Fescue

4 *Coreopsis palmata*   Tickseed
  Bromus secalinus   Cheat, Chess
  Smilacina racemosa   False Spikenard
  Hordeum jubatum   Squirrel-Tail Grass

5 *Cyperus rivularis*   Brook-Sedge

6 *Carex stricta*   Sedge

7 *Cyperus esculentus*   Yellow Nut-Grass
  Cyperus sp.   Nut-Grass, Umbrella-Sedge
  Cynodon dactylon   Bermuda-Grass

8 *Allium stellatum*   Wild Onion

9 *Erythronium albidum*   White Trout-Lily,
  White Dogtooth-Violet

10 *Zephyranthes rosea*   Zephyr-Lily

11 *Hypoxis hirsuta*   Star-Grass
   Sisyrinchium campestre   Blue-Eyed Grass

12 *Cypripedium arietinum*   Ram's-Head Lady-Slipper

13 *Cypripedium calceolus* L. var. *pubescens*
   Large Yellow Lady-Slipper

14 *Cypripedium candidum*   White Lady-Slipper

15 *Cypripedium reginae*   Showy Lady-Slipper

16 *Cypripedium reginae*   Showy Lady-Slipper

17 *Platanthera praeclara*   Prairie White Fringed Orchid

18 *Pogonia ophioglossoides*   Rose Pogonia

19 *Calopogon tuberosus*   Grass-Pink, Swamp-Pink
   Potentilla palustris   Marsh-Cinquefoil

20 *Arethusa bulbosa*   Dragon's-Mouth

21 *Populus deltoides*   Cottonwood
   Betula papyrifera   Paper-Birch, Canoe-Birch

22 *Asarum canadense*   Wild Ginger

23 *Ranunculus rhomboideus*   Prairie-Buttercup
Fragaria virginiana   Strawberry

24 *Pulsatilla nuttalliana*   Pasque-Flower

25 *Parnassia palustris* L. var. *neogaea*
Grass-of-Parnassus
Cirsium muticum   Swamp-Thistle

26 *Pyrus ioensis*   Wild Crab

27 *Rubus strigosus*   American Red Raspberry

28 *Petalostemon purpureum*   Purple Prairie-Clover

29 *Hibiscus militaris*   Halberd-leaved Rose-Mallow

30 *Viola cucullata*   Violet
Cyperus rivularis   Brook-Sedge

31 *Viola pedatifida*   Bird-Foot Violet

32 *Gentianella quinquefolia*
Gentianopsis crinita   Fringed Gentian
Rhus glabra   Smooth Sumac

33 *Gentiana puberulenta*   Prairie Gentian

34 *Gentiana andrewsii*   Closed Gentian, Bottle-Gentian

35 *Gentiana andrewsii*   Closed Gentian, Bottle-Gentian
Parnassia palustris L. var. *neogaea*
Grass-of-Parnassus

36 *Lycium barbatum*   Common Matrimony-Vine
Bouteloua gracilis   Grama-Grass

37 *Penstemon grandiflorus*   Beard-Tongue

38 *Pinguicula vulgaris*   Butterwort

39 *Asperula orientalis*   Woodruff

40 *Lobelia cardinalis*   Cardinal-Flower

41 *Lobelia siphilitica*   Great Lobelia

42 *Aster* sp.
Boltonia sp.

43 *Helianthus maximiliani*   Sunflower

44 *Chrysanthemum leucanthemum*   Ox-Eye Daisy

45 *Emilia javanica*   Tassel Flower
Boltonia asteroides

46 *Cirsium discolor*   Common Thistle

PLATE 1

Sagittaria graminea Michx. *(left)*

Sagittaria latifolia Willd. *(right)*
Duck-Potato, Wapato

Sagittaria latifolia, Willd.
Arrowhead
Minnesota 1875

The tubers on the fibrous roots of the Duck-Potato (called also Swan Potato by the Ojibway Indians), common plant of wet places, are sometimes as large as a hen's egg and were a favorite and important native food source. As the vernacular names indicate, aquatic fowl apparently also find them palatable. The popular name Arrowhead used by Terry, and still widely in use today, refers to the arrow-shaped or lanceolate leaf blade.

Although Terry assigns the flowers in her painting to a single species of *Sagittaria,* the flowering stalks in fact represent two different species of the genus: *S. graminea* and *S. latifolia.*

PLATE 2

Bouteloua hirsuta Lag.
Grama-Grass

Bouteloua curtipendula (Michx.) Torr.
Side-Oats Grama

Bouteloua hirsuta, Lag.
Bouteloua curtipendula, Michx.
Minnesota 1878

In his catalogue of the flora of Minnesota Upham listed
these two grama-grasses among "the most abundant species
of grass found upon the prairies of southwestern Minnesota."

PLATE 3

Vulpia octoflora (Walt.) Rydb.
Six-Weeks Fescue

Festuca pratensis Hudson
Meadow-Fescue

Festuca octoflora, Walt.
Festuca elatior, L.
Minnesota 1879

87

Coreopsis palmata Nutt.
Tickseed

Bromus secalinus L.
Cheat, Chess

Smilacina racemosa (L.) Desf.
False Spikenard

Hordeum jubatum L.
Squirrel-Tail Grass

Coreopsis lanceolata, L.
Bromus secalinus, L.
Smilacina racemosa, L.
Hordeum jubatum, L.
[with dragonfly and wild raspberry]
[signed] E. H. T.
Minnesota 1878

Terry's Tickseed appears to be *Coreopsis palmata* rather than *C. lanceolata*. In some instances the nomenclature Terry uses has become obsolete; in this case the name change suggests a misidentification.

Cyperus rivularis Kunth
Brook-Sedge

Cyperus rivularis, Kunth.
Minnesota 1878

PLATE 6

Carex stricta Lam.
Sedge

Carex stricta, Lam.
Minnesota 1878

PLATE 7

Cyperus esculentus L.
Yellow Nut-Grass

Cyperus sp.
Nut-Grass, Umbrella-Sedge

Cynodon dactylon (L.) Pers.
Bermuda-Grass

Cyperus esculentus, L.
Scirpus sp.
Cynodon Dactylon, L.
Bermuda Grass
Minnesota 1878

Perhaps Terry found all three of these species in a Minnesota garden. The perennial grass *Cynodon*, native in Europe, Asia, and Australia, is well adapted to garden, landscape, or border planting. Species of *Cyperus* are frequently cultivated. The specimen Terry has identified as a *Scirpus* is actually a species of *Cyperus*.

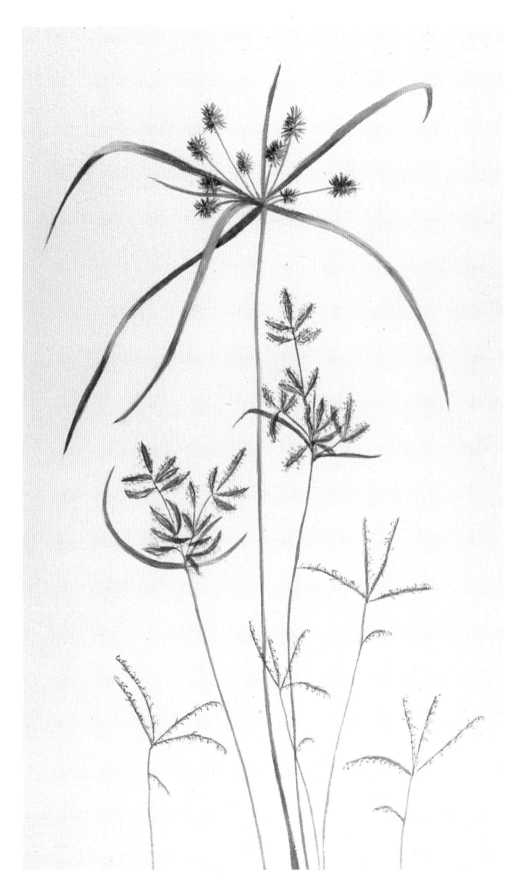

PLATE 8

Allium stellatum Ker
Wild Onion

Allium stellatum, Ker.
Wild Onion
Minnesota 1878

Terry may have painted the Wild Onion in Alexandria,
Minnesota. Upham recorded her collection of it there.

PLATE 9

Erythronium albidum Nutt.
White Trout-Lily, White Dogtooth-Violet

Erythronium albidum, Nutt.
White Dog-tooth Violet
Minnesota 1876

Zephyranthes rosea Lindl.
Zephyr-Lily

Zephyranthes rosea, Lindl.
Fairy Lily
Minnesota 1878

The Zephyr-Lily is one of the few cultivated species Terry painted while in Minnesota. Since the bulbs will not survive Minnesota winters in the garden, it is generally grown as a houseplant.

Hypoxis hirsuta (L.) Cov.
Star-Grass

Sisyrinchium campestre Bickn.
Blue-Eyed Grass

Hypoxis hirsuta, L.
Star Grass
Sisyrinchium gramineum, Curtis
Blue-eyed Grass
Minnesota 1875

The Blue-Eyed Grass Terry has identified as *Sisyrinchium gramineum* appears to be in fact *S. campestre*. The change in specific name here indicates a misidentification rather than a change in nomenclature.

Cypripedium arietinum R. Br.
Ram's-Head Lady-Slipper

Cypripedium arietinum, R. Br.
Ram's-head Moccasin Flower
Clearwater, Minnesota 1878

Upham documented Terry's collection of the Ram's-Head
Lady-Slipper thus: "Clearwater Lake, in the northwest part
of Wright county, *Mrs. Terry.*" He called it rare. This orchid, described as legendary, is at present considered an
endangered species in Minnesota; Upham's "rare" now
approaches "extremely rare." In fact, Terry's painting is a
memento of a population now gone: we are told that the
Ram's-Head has not been seen in Wright County since
1927. So we look at Terry's rendition with some sadness,
a reminder of something that once was. And that sadness
is anything but relieved as we read further in Coffin and
Pfannmuller's account of Minnesota's endangered flora and
fauna: "Many of the remaining populations [of *Cypripedium arietinum*] face a critical threat from orchid fanciers
who selfishly and illicitly dig up these plants, even in state
parks and state scientific and natural areas. This type of
poaching is especially tragic because the plants do not survive transplantation from the wild."

PLATE 13

Cypripedium calceolus L.
var. *pubescens* (Willd.) Correll
Large Yellow Lady-Slipper

Cypripedium parviflorum,
var. *pubescens*—Knight
Larger Yellow Lady's Slipper
Minnesota 1875

"Common, or frequent, throughout the state," Upham noted of the Large Yellow Lady-Slipper. More than one hundred years later this statement still describes the occurrence of the species in Minnesota.

PLATE 14

Cypripedium candidum Muhl. ex Willd.
White Lady-Slipper

Cypripedium candidum, Muhl.
Small White Lady's Slipper
Minnesota 1878

Terry collected the White Lady-Slipper in the Lake Harriet area of Minneapolis. Upham documented its occurrence throughout a large area of Minnesota. Even though the species has declined significantly in the state because of the severe reduction of its prairie habitat, it is today not considered rare here. However, since Minnesota is a stronghold for the species, it is important that its survival be assured. To this end Coffin and Pfannmuller consider it a species of special concern.

Cypripedium reginae Walt.
Showy Lady-Slipper

Cypripedium hirsutum, Mill.
Showy Lady's Slipper
Minnesota 1875

This painting is believed to be the first illustration of the Showy Lady-Slipper in the state of Minnesota. After several years of botanical uncertainty, the species was designated the official Minnesota state flower or "floral emblem" in 1902. The Minnesota legislature in 1925 passed a law protecting the lady-slippers and other orchids, as well as various other wildflowers.

PLATE 16

Cypripedium reginae Walt.
Showy Lady-Slipper

Cypripedium hirsutum, Mill.
Showy Lady's Slipper
Studies of buds
Minnesota 1878

Platanthera praeclara Sheviak & Bowles
Prairie White Fringed Orchid

Habenaria leucophaea, Nutt.
Rein Orchis
Minnesota 1875

Terry's collection of this orchid, along with his own, allowed Upham to describe its distribution in Minnesota in
the early 1880s as follows: "Frequent in the south half of
the state, extending north at least to Alexandria, *Mrs. Terry,*
and Clay County, in the Red River valley, *Upham.*" More
recent collections extend its range in Minnesota as far north
as Polk County. However, Coffin and Pfannmuller cate-
gorize this species as endangered in the state because of its
reduction to critically low numbers throughout its range.

PLATE 18

Pogonia ophioglossoides (L.) Juss.
Rose Pogonia

Pogonia ophioglossoides, Ker.
Minnesota 1876

Apparently this orchid was readily seen in the urban area of
Minnesota in Terry's day. Upham cited it as "frequent" in
Minneapolis; Terry found it in St. Paul.

Calopogon tuberosus (L.) BSP.
Grass-Pink, Swamp-Pink

Potentilla palustris (L.) Scop.
Marsh-Cinquefoil

Calopogon pulchellus, R. Br.
Grass Pink
Potentilla palustris, L.
Minnesota 1878

Both these species were common, or frequent, throughout Minnesota when Terry painted them. The Marsh-
Cinquefoil remains so today; the orchid Grass-Pink is now
less frequently seen.

PLATE 20

Arethusa bulbosa L.
Dragon's-Mouth

Arethusa bulbosa, L.
Arethusa
Minnesota 1877

The orchid Dragon's-Mouth of northern Minnesota was considered rare when Terry painted it in 1877. Although the species is not considered rare in Minnesota today, some protection should nevertheless be accorded it since it is known to be declining over a significant portion of its range.

⚜

P L A T E   2 1

Populus deltoides Marsh.
Cottonwood

Betula papyrifera Marsh.
Paper-Birch, Canoe-Birch

Populus deltoides, Marsh
Cotton-wood
Betula lenta, L.
Black Birch
Minnesota 1878

When Terry painted this study of birch and cottonwood
catkins, the distribution of *Betula lenta* had not been completely determined. Some workers believed the species possibly extended west to northern Minnesota. It is now clear,
however, that the Black Birch is not a Minnesota species.
The warm brown ascending branchlets of Terry's specimens, with their young, slender, erect catkins, make it highly probable that Terry's birch was in fact *Betula papyrifera*
Marsh., the Paper- or Canoe-Birch.

PLATE 22

Asarum canadense L.
Wild Ginger

Asarum Canadense, L.
Wild Ginger
Minnesota 1876

The Ojibway Indians of Minnesota and elsewhere used the rhizome and roots of Wild Ginger for medicinal purposes (to treat indigestion) and for flavoring their food.

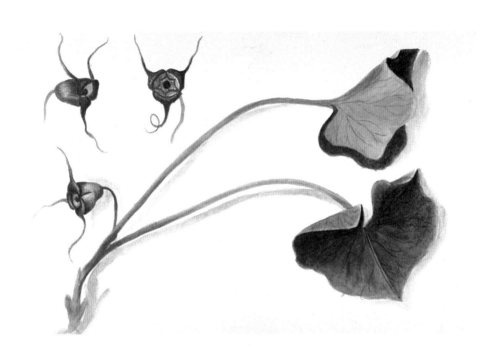

PLATE 23

Ranunculus rhomboideus Goldie
Prairie-Buttercup

Fragaria virginiana Duchesne
Strawberry

Ranunculus rhomboideus, Goldie
Dwarf Buttercup
Fragaria Virginiana, Duchesne
Wild Strawberry
Minnesota 1875

Pulsatilla nuttalliana (DC.) Bercht. & J. S. Presl
Pasque-Flower

Anemone patens, L.
Pasque Flower
Minnesota 1875

In Terry's day this earliest flower of spring was known by
an unusual variety of popular names in addition to Pasque
Flower: Hartshorn-plant, Headache-plant, Gosling, Prairie
Smoke, and Crocus.

Parnassia palustris L. var. *neogaea* Fern.
Grass-of-Parnassus

Cirsium muticum Michx.
Swamp-Thistle

Parnassia palustris, L.
Grass of Parnassus
Cirsium muticum, Michx.
Thistle
Minnesota 1875

PLATE 26

Pyrus ioensis (Wood) Carruth.
Wild Crab

Malus Ioensis, Bailey
Wild Apple
Minnesota 1878

PLATE 27

Rubus strigosus Michx.
American Red Raspberry

Rubus idaeus.
Wild Red Raspberry
Minnesota 1878

PLATE 28

Petalostemon purpureum (Vent.) Rydb.
Purple Prairie-Clover

Petalostemum purpureum, Rydb.
Prairie Clover
Minnesota 1878

Upham noted that Purple Prairie-Clover was "abundant in all the prairie portion of the state [Minnesota]." With the marked decline over the intervening years of habitat suitable for this species, we can safely conjecture that Terry saw much larger stands of it than we do today.

Hibiscus militaris Cav.
Halberd-leaved Rose-Mallow

Hibiscus militaris, Cav.
Halberd-leaved Rose Mallow
Minnesota 1878

Upham documented Terry's collection of this species: "Banks of the Mississippi river between Saint Paul and Mendota (abundant). *Mrs. Terry.*"

Viola cucullata Ait.
Violet

Cyperus rivularis Kunth
Brook-Sedge

Viola cucullata, Ait.
Blue Violet
Lake Park, Sept. 18, 1880
Cyperus rivularis, Kunth.
Minnesota 1880

Viola pedatifida G. Don
Bird-Foot Violet

Viola pedatifida, G. Don.
Violet
Minnesota 1875

PLATE 32

Gentianella quinquefolia (L.) Small

Gentianopsis crinita (Froel.) Ma
Fringed Gentian

Rhus glabra L.
Smooth Sumac

Gentiana quinquefolia, L.
Gentiana crinita, Froel.
Fringed Gentian
Rhus glabra, L.
Sumach
Minnesota 1878

P L A T E   3 3

Gentiana puberulenta Pringle
Prairie Gentian

Gentiana puberula, Michx.
Gentian
Minnesota 1876

PLATE 34

Gentiana andrewsii Griseb.
Closed Gentian, Bottle-Gentian

Gentiana Andrewsii, Griseb.
Closed Gentian
Minnesota 1878

Gentiana andrewsii Griseb.
Closed Gentian, Bottle-Gentian

Parnassia palustris L. var. *neogaea* Fern.
Grass-of-Parnassus

Gentiana Andrewsii, Griseb.
Closed Gentian
Parnassia palustris, L.
Grass of Parnassus
Minnesota 1878

P L A T E   3 6

Lycium barbatum L.
Common Matrimony-Vine

Bouteloua gracilis (HBK.) Lag. ex Steud.
Grama-Grass

Lycium halimifolium, Mill.
Matrimony Vine
Bouteloua oligostachya, Nutt.
Mesquite Grass
An aerial visitor, and an example of
protective coloring in the spider.
Minnesota 1878

Penstemon grandiflorus Nutt.
Beard-Tongue

Pentstemon grandiflorus, Nutt.
Beard Tongue
Campus of the University of Minnesota 1875

Pinguicula vulgaris L.
Butterwort

Pinguicula vulgaris, L.
Butterwort
Minnesota 1876

This plant is found in Minnesota—as it was in the 1870s—
only along the north shore of Lake Superior, where it grows
on wet, calcareous rocks. The soft-fleshy leaves, which form
a basal cluster, are mostly greasy to the touch, from which
the genus derives its name (*pinguis,* fat).

PLATE 39

Asperula orientalis Boiss and Hohen.
Woodruff

Asperula orientalis, Boiss and Hohen.
Minnesota 1875

Woodruffs are grown in borders or rock gardens where
they thrive in shady places, although A. *orientalis* does well
in the open garden.

PLATE 40

Lobelia cardinalis L.
Cardinal-Flower

Lobelia cardinalis, L.
Cardinal Flower
[with an aster and a grass]
Minnesota 1878

Terry collected the Cardinal-Flower along the Mississippi
River at St. Paul.

Lobelia siphilitica L.
Great Lobelia

Lobelia syphilitica, L.
Great Blue Lobelia
[with polygonums and a grass]
Minnesota 1878

163

PLATE 42

Aster sp.
Boltonia sp.

Aster and Boltonia
Minnesota 1878

Upham recorded Terry's collections of Boltonia and ten species of Aster in Douglas County, Minnesota. Perhaps these collections furnished the subjects for this painting.

Helianthus maximiliani Schrad.
Sunflower

Helianthus Maximiliani, Schrad.
Wild Sunflower
Minnesota 1878

This sunflower, called by some Maximilian's Sunflower, is named after Prince Maximilian von Wied-Neuwied, who discovered it when he traveled over the plains and prairies of America in the early nineteenth century. Upham described it as "continuing as the most troublesome weed in wheat-fields." And added further, "The most noteworthy member of this genus in Minnesota."

PLATE 44

Chrysanthemum leucanthemum L.
Ox-Eye Daisy

Chrysanthemum Leucanthemum, L.
Ox-eye Daisy
Minnesota 1878

In his catalogue Upham noted collections of the Ox-Eye Daisy from many widespread sites in Minnesota, but described it as "rare or local." "Inclined to spread," he warned, and added, "an abundant and pernicious weed in states farther east."

Emilia javanica (Burm. f.) C. B. Robins.
Tassel Flower

Boltonia asteroides (L.) L'Her.

Cacalia coccinea, L.
Tassel Flower
Boltonia latisquama, Gray
Minnesota 1876

The scarlet-headed Tassel Flower, cultivated as a flower-garden annual, is a native of the Old World tropics. Upham noted Terry's collection of Boltonia in Alexandria, Minnesota, as one of the northern records for the species.

PLATE 46

Cirsium discolor (Muhl.) Spreng.
Common Thistle

Cirsium discolor, Muhl.
Thistle
Minnesota 1875

Descriptive Catalogue
of the Paintings

ALTHOUGH ONLY TERRY'S PAINTINGS OF THE MINnesota flora and a few of her early works are reproduced here, the accompanying tabular catalogue lists in alphabetical order all the species illustrated and identified in the entire collection. The size of each painting is noted, as well as where and when it was done. Plant nomenclature is given exactly as reported by Terry. Signatures are recorded if present. All information furnished by Terry is contained in the tabulation, including her occasional explanatory notes. For the sake of clarity, some words have been added in the catalogue that do not appear with the paintings. Such material is always enclosed in brackets.

Two additional summaries, in which the paintings and the species illustrated are listed according to state and date, are provided to make the statistical data about the paintings more readily accessible.

Descriptive Catalogue of *American Flowers*

Painted by Mrs. Emily Hitchcock Terry

Scientific name, common name, and notes	Size (inches)	Place and date
Actaea rubra, Willd. Red Baneberry	6⅜ x 11⅞	Dorset, Vermont 1893
Allamanda Williamsi Allamanda Greenhouse in Agricultural College	6¾ x 12¼	Amherst [Massachusetts] 1870
Allium stellatum, Ker. Wild Onion	6¾ x 9⅞	Minnesota 1878
Andropogon furcatus, Muhl. [with] *Bromus ciliatus,* L., *Chrysopogon nutans,* Benth., Wheat with and without the awns	8½ x 11¾	[Place and date not given]
Anemone patens, L. Pasque Flower	5⅝ x 9⅞	Minnesota 1875
Anemone patens, L. Pasque Flower	6⅜ x 9⅞	Colorado Springs [Colorado] 1878
Anemonella thalictroides, L. Rue Anemone	5¾ x 10	Northampton [Massachusetts] 1895
Anogra albicaulis, Pursh. White Evening Primrose	6⅞ x 9⅞	Colorado Springs [Colorado] 1878
Aplectrum hyemale, Nutt. My first painting from nature. Done in Amherst 1850. From "The Notch," Mt. Holyoke	6½ x 11	Amherst [Massachusetts] 1850
[Apple flower buds] From the Bud to the Fruit Painted in the Pre-Raphaelite Class at Cooper Institute in New York 1867 [Signed] E. Hitchcock 1866	4⅝ x 4⅝	New York [City] 1866/1867
[Apple fruit] From the Bud to the Fruit From the home of William Cullen Bryant in Cummington	5 x 5⅜	Cummington [Massachusetts] 1867
Aquilegia Canadensis, L. Columbine	5⅜ x 10	Northampton [Massachusetts] 1879
Arctostaphylos Uva-ursi, L. Bearberry	6¾ x 10	Colorado Springs [Colorado] 1878
Arethusa bulbosa, L. Arethusa	4⅞ x 10	Minnesota 1877
Asarum arifolium, Michx. Wild Ginger	6⅞ x 5⅛	Aiken, South Carolina 1881
Asarum Canadense, L. Wild Ginger	9⅞ x 5⅞	Minnesota 1876
Asperula orientalis, Boiss and Hohen.	6⅞ x 9⅞	Minnesota 1875
Aster [sp.] and *Boltonia* [sp.]	4⅞ x 9¼	Minnesota 1878
Aster puniceus, L. Purple Aster	5⅞ x 8⅞	Chautauqua Co. N. Y. 1870
Betula lenta, L. Black Birch [with] *Populus deltoides,* Marsh Cottonwood	6⅝ x 11⅞	Minnesota 1878

Scientific name, common name, and notes	Size (inches)	Place and date
Bidens cernua, L. Bur Marigold	6 x 8⅞	Chautauqua Co. N. Y. 1870
Bignonia capreolata, L. Cross-vine [Signed] E. H. Terry	6⅞ x 12	St. Augustine, Florida 1879
Boltonia [sp.] (see *Aster* [sp.])		
Boltonia latisquama, Gray [with] *Cacalia coccinea,* L. Tassel Flower	6½ x 11¾	Minnesota 1876
Bossekia deliciosa, A. Nels. False Raspberry	6⅞ x 9⅞	Colorado Springs [Colorado] 1878
Bouteloua curtipendula, Michx. [with] *Bouteloua hirsuta,* Lag.	5 x 10⅞	Minnesota 1878
Bouteloua hirsuta, Lag. (see *Bouteloua curtipendula*, Michx.)		
Bouteloua oligostachya, Nutt. Mesquite Grass [with] *Lycium halimifolium,* Mill. Matrimony Vine An aerial visitor [dragonfly], and an example of protective coloring in the spider	5⅞ x 10	Minnesota 1878
Bromus ciliatus, L. (see *Andropogon furcatus*, Muhl.)		
Bromus secalinus, L. [with] *Coreopsis lanceolata,* L., *Hordeum jubatum,* L., *Smilacina racemosa,* L. [with dragonfly] [Signed] E. H. T.	7 x 12	Minnesota 1878
Cacalia coccinea, L. (see *Boltonia latisquama,* Gray)		
Calopogon pulchellus, R. Br. Grass Pink [with] *Potentilla palustris,* L.	6¼ x 14¾	Minnesota 1878
Caltha palustris, L. Marsh Marigold	5½ x 9⅞	Amherst [Massachusetts] 1870
Camellia Japonica, L. Done in the Pre-Raphaelite Class at Cooper Institute in New York 1866 It took the first prize [Signed] E. Hitchcock 1866	8¼ x 9½	New York [City] 1866
Campanula rotundifolia, L. Harebell	6 x 8⅞	Chautauqua Co. N. Y. 1870
Campanula rotundifolia, L. Harebell	4⅛ x 10⅞	Dorset, Vermont 1900
Carex stricta, Lam.	6½ x 11⅞	Minnesota 1878
Castilleia coccinea, Spreng. Painted Cup	6⅞ x 10	Amherst [Massachusetts] 1870
Castilleja integra. Painted Cup	6½ x 9⅞	Colorado Springs [Colorado] 1878
Centaurea Cyanus, L. Bachelor's Buttons	8¾ x 12⅞	Dorset, Vermont 1893
Chrysanthemum Indicum. Done in the Pre-Raphaelite Class at Cooper Institute in New York 1866 [Signed] E. Hitchcock 1866	6¼ x 9	New York [City] 1866

Scientific name, common name, and notes	Size (inches)	Place and date
Chrysanthemum Leucanthemum, L. Ox-eye Daisy	5⅞ x 9¾	Minnesota 1878
Chrysopogon nutans, Benth. (see *Andropogon furcatus*, Muhl.)		
Cirsium discolor, Muhl. Thistle	7 x 10	Minnesota 1875
Cirsium muticum, Michx. Thistle [with] *Parnassia palustris*, L. Grass of Parnassus	6⅞ x 11⅞	Minnesota 1875
Clematis pseudoalpina, A. Nels. Clematis	6¼ x 10	Colorado Springs [Colorado] 1878
Clematis pseudoalpina, A. Nels. Clematis	6⅞ x 9⅞	Colorado Springs [Colorado] 1878
Clematis Viticella, L. Cultivated Clematis	5⅛ x 14	Amherst [Massachusetts] 1870
Clover, A Four-leaved	5⅝ x 8⅞	Chautauqua Co. N. Y. 1870
Convolvulus sepium, L. Hedge Bindweed	6 x 8⅞	Chautauqua Co. N. Y. 1870
Coreopsis lanceolata, L. (see *Bromus secalinus* L.)		
Coreopsis tinctoria, Nutt. Coreopsis [with] *Melilotus alba*, Desr. Sweet Clover [Signed] E. H. T.	5¾ x 10	Dorset, Vermont 1895
Cornus florida, L. Dogwood [Signed] E. H. Terry '83.	10 x 14	Orange, New Jersey 1883
Cyclamen Europaeum, L. Cyclamen	6⅞ x 11⅞	Northampton [Massachusetts] 1890
Cynodon Dactylon, L. Bermuda Grass [with] *Cyperus esculentus*, L., *Scirpus* sp.	6⅞ x 11⅞	Minnesota 1878
Cyperus esculentus, L. (see *Cynodon Dactylon*, L.)		
Cyperus rivularis, Kunth.	5¾ x 8¾	Minnesota 1878
Cyperus rivularis, Kunth. [with] *Viola cucullata*, Ait. Blue Violet Lake Park, Sept. 18, 1880	6⅞ x 12	Minnesota 1880
Cypripedium acaule, Ait. Stemless Lady's Slipper	6¾ x 11⅞	Northampton [Massachusetts] 1886
Cypripedium arietinum, R. Br. Ram's-head Moccasin Flower	5½ x 10	Clearwater, Minnesota 1878
Cypripedium candidum, Muhl. Small White Lady's Slipper	5⅞ x 10	Minnesota 1878
Cypripedium hirsutum, Mill. Showy Lady's Slipper	10¼ x14⅛	Minnesota 1875
Cypripedium hirsutum, Mill. Showy Lady's Slipper	4⅝ x 9½	Minnesota 1878

Scientific name, common name, and notes	Size (inches)	Place and date
Cypripedium hirsutum, Mill. Showy Lady's Slipper, Studies of buds	6¾ x 9⅞	Minnesota 1878
Cypripedium parviflorum, var. *pubescens,* Knight Larger Yellow Lady's Slipper Gathered on Mt. Holyoke	6⅝ x 12	Amherst [Massachusetts] 1870
Cypripedium parviflorum, var. *pubescens*—Knight Larger Yellow Lady's Slipper	5⅞ x 10	Minnesota 1875
Deutzia scabra, Thunb. Deutzia [Signed] E. H. T.	6 x 10½	Aiken, South Carolina 1881
Dichromena latifolia, Baldw.	6⅜ x 11⅞	Aiken, South Carolina 1881
Erigeron annuus, L. Fleabane	6⅞ x 10	Northampton [Massachusetts] 1890
Erigeron Philadelphicus, L. (pink) [with] *Erigeron pulchellus,* Michx. (blue) Robin's Plantain	10¾ x 15	Northampton [Massachusetts] 1892
Erigeron pulchellus, Michx. (see *Erigeron Philadelphicus,* L.)		
Erigeron uniflorus, L. Erigeron/Fleabane	9⅞ x 6⅞	Colorado Springs [Colorado] 1878
Eriophorum callitrix, Cham. Cotton Grass	2⅝ x 14⅝	Dorset, Vermont 1900
Erythronium albidum, Nutt. White Dog-tooth Violet	5⅝ x 10	Minnesota 1876
Fagus grandifolia, Ehrb. Beech	8⅜ x 12¼	Vermont 1900
Festuca elatior, L. [with] *Festuca octoflora,* Walt.	5½ x 10	Minnesota 1879
Festuca octoflora, Walt. (see *Festuca elatior,* L.)		
Fragaria Virginiana, Duchesne Wild Strawberry [with] *Ranunculus rhomboideus,* Goldie Dwarf Buttercup	4⅞ x 10	Minnesota 1875
Gelsemium sempervirens, Ait. Yellow Jessamine	6⅜ x 11⅞	St. Augustine, Florida 1878
Gelsemium sempervirens, Ait. Yellow Jessamine	5¾ x 10	Aiken, South Carolina 1881
Gelsemium sempervirens, L. Yellow Jessamine [with] *Lonicera sempervirens,* L. Trumpet Honeysuckle	6¾ x 15	Aiken, South Carolina 1881
Gentiana Andrewsii, Griseb. Closed Gentian	7 x 12	Minnesota 1878
Gentiana Andrewsii, Griseb. Closed Gentian [with] *Parnassia palustris,* L. Grass of Parnassus	6⅞ x 10	Minnesota 1878

Scientific name, common name, and notes	Size (inches)	Place and date
Gentiana Andrewsii, Griseb. Closed Gentian [with four butterflies]	7¼ x 8⅝	Vermont 1900
Gentiana crinita, Froel. Fringed Gentian [with] *Gentiana quinquefolia,* L., *Rhus glabra,* L. Sumach	6⅞ x 11⅞	Minnesota 1878
Gentiana crinita, Froel. Fringed Gentian [with] *Lobelia cardinalis,* L. Cardinal Flower Painted in Amherst (when only a child)	8⅞ x 12	Amherst [Massachusetts] [date not given]
Gentiana puberula, Michx. Gentian	10½ x 14⅞	Minnesota 1876
Gentiana quinquefolia, L. (see *Gentiana crinita*, Froel.)		
Habenaria leucophaea, Nutt. Rein Orchis	6⅛ x 15½	Minnesota 1875
Helianthus Maximiliani, Schrad. Wild Sunflower	6⅞ x 13½	Minnesota 1878
Hibiscus militaris, Cav. Halberd-leaved Rose Mallow	7½ x 7⅜	Minnesota 1878
Hibiscus Rosa-Sinensis, L. Rose of China	6⅞ x 9⅞	Amherst [Massachusetts] 1870
Hippeastrum Johnsoni Amaryllis	8⅞ x 14⅜	Northampton [Massachusetts] 1879
Hordeum jubatum, L. (see *Bromus secalinus*, L.)		
Hypoxis hirsuta, L. Star Grass [with] *Sisyrinchium gramineum,* Curtis Blue-eyed Grass	5⅞ x 11¾	Minnesota 1875
Ipomoea purpurea, L. Morning Glory	5¾ x 8⅞	Chautauqua Co. N. Y. 1870
Iris verna, L. Dwarf Iris	5 x 7	Aiken, South Carolina 1881
Lathyrus odoratus, L. Sweet Peas	6¾ x 12	Dorset, Vermont 1892
Lathyrus ornatus, Nutt.	6⅞ x 9⅞	Colorado Springs [Colorado] 1878
Leucocrinum montanum, Nutt. White Mountain Lily	6½ x 9¾	Colorado Springs [Colorado] 1878
[Lichens, ferns, and other species] Growing on a piece of decayed wood [Signed] E. H. 1868	12 x 7⅞	Bethlehem, N. H. 1868
Lilium philadelphicum, L. Wild Orange-red Lily	6¾ x 11⅞	Amherst [Massachusetts] 1870
Lilium superbum, L. Turk's Cap Lily	8¾ x 13⅞	Amherst [Massachusetts] 1868
Lobelia cardinalis, L. Cardinal Flower [with an aster and a grass]	6¾ x 15	Minnesota 1878
Lobelia cardinalis, L. (see *Gentiana crinita*, Froel.)		

Scientific name, common name, and notes	Size (inches)	Place and date
Lobelia syphilitica, L. Great Blue Lobelia [with other species]	7 x 15	Minnesota 1878
Lonicera sempervirens, Ait. Trumpet Honeysuckle [with] *Viola pedata*, L. var. *lineariloba*, D. C. Bird-foot Violet [Signed] Aiken, Apr. 13, 1881 E. H. T.	5⅞ x 10	Aiken, South Carolina 1881
Lonicera sempervirens, L. (see *Gelsemium sempervirens*, L.)		
Lycium halimifolium, Mill. (see *Bouteloua oligostachya*, Nutt.)		
Malus Ioensis, Bailey Wild Apple	5⅛ x 7	Minnesota 1878
Melilotus alba, Desr. (see *Coreopsis tinctoria*, Nutt.)		
Mertensia cynoglossoides, Greene Lungwort	5⅞ x 9⅞	Colorado Springs [Colorado] 1878
Oxytropis Lamberti, Pursh.	6¾ x 9⅞	Colorado Springs [Colorado] 1878
Papaver glaucum, Boiss. Poppy	6 x 9	Chautauqua Co. N. Y. 1870
Papaver Rhoeas, L. Corn Poppy	9¼ x 13	Dorset, Vermont 1900
Parnassia palustris, L. (see *Cirsium muticum*, Michx.)		
Parnassia palustris, L. (see *Gentiana Andrewsii*, Griseb.)		
Passiflora lutea, L. Passion Flower	5½ x 10⅞	Aiken, South Carolina 1881
Pentstemon angustifolius, Pursh. Blue Beard-Tongue	7 x 9⅞	Colorado Springs [Colorado] 1878
Pentstemon grandiflorus, Nutt. Beard Tongue Campus of the University of Minnesota 1875	5½ x 10⅛	Minnesota 1875
Petalostemum purpureum, Rydb. Prairie Clover	5¼ x 9	Minnesota 1876
Petalostemum purpureum, Rydb. Prairie Clover	4 x 6¾	Minnesota 1878
Pinguicula vulgaris, L. Butterwort	6⅞ x 12	Minnesota 1876
Plumbago Capensis, Thunb. Leadwort	5¾ x 10	Aiken, South Carolina 1881
Pogonia divaricata, R. Br. This painting was sent to Mr. Oakes Ames who considered it of sufficient value to extend the range to Florida, where it was painted in 1875.	6 x 10½	Florida 1875
Pogonia ophioglossoides, Ker.	3⅝ x 11¾	Minnesota 1876

Scientific name, common name, and notes	Size (inches)	Place and date
Pogonia verticillata, Nutt.	5¼ x 10⅞	Amherst [Massachusetts] 1854
Polygala polygama, Walt.	6¾ x 9⅝	Aiken, South Carolina 1881
Populus deltoides, Marsh (see *Betula lenta*, L.)		
Potentilla palustris, L. (see *Calopogon pulchellus*, R. Br.)		
Prunus Persica, L. Peach [with] *Utricularia inflata*, Walt. Bladderwort	6⅞ x 9⅞	Minnesota 1878 [Labeling error; probably Florida]
Psoralea argophylla, Pursh.	6¾ x 9⅝	Colorado Springs [Colorado] 1878
Punica Granatum, L. Pomegranate	6¾ x 12	St. Augustine, Florida 1876
Pyrus Japonica, Thunb. Japanese Pear [Signed] E. H. T.	5⅛ x 10¾	Aiken, South Carolina 1881
Ranunculus acris, L. Buttercups	5¾ x 8⅝	Chautauqua Co. N. Y. 1870
Ranunculus rhomboideus, Goldie (see *Fragaria Virginiana*, Duchesne)		
Rhinanthus Crista galli, L. Rattle box Found in Vermont for the first time in June 1910 at Bennington By E. H. Terry [unmounted; notes written on back]	5 x 11¼	Bennington [Vermont] 1910
Rhododendron nudiflorum, L. Swamp Pink	6 x 8⅞	Chautauqua Co. N. Y. 1870
Rhus glabra, L. Sumach Leaf in autumn coloring	4¼ x 7	Amherst [Massachusetts] 1869
Rhus glabra, L. (see *Gentiana crinita*, Froel.)		
Rosa laevigata, Michx. Cherokee Rose [Signed] E. H. T.	5¼ x 10⅞	St. Augustine, Florida 1876
Rubus idaeus Wild Red Raspberry	6⅞ x 10	Minnesota 1878
Sagittaria latifolia, Willd. Arrowhead	6¾ x 10¼	Minnesota 1875
Sarracenia flava, L. Trumpets	6⅝ x 11⅞	St. Augustine, Florida 1878
Schrankia uncinata, Willd. Sensitive Brier	6⅞ x 11⅞	Aiken, South Carolina 1881
Scirpus sp. (see *Cynodon Dactylon*, L.)		
Scutellaria Brittonii, Porter Skullcap	6¾ x 9⅞	Colorado Springs [Colorado] 1878
Sisyrinchium gramineum, Curtis (see *Hypoxis hirsuta*, L.)		
Smilacina racemosa, L. (see *Bromus secalinus*, L.)		
Tecoma jasminoides, Lindl.	6⅜ x 11⅞	St. Augustine, Florida 1878

Scientific name, common name, and notes	Size (inches)	Place and date
Tecoma radicans, L. Trumpet Flower [Signed] E. H. Terry '83.	10⅜ x 14¼	Painesville, Ohio 1883
Tephrosia Virginiana, L. Goat's Rue	6 x 9⅞	Aiken, South Carolina 1881
Thermopsis rhombifolia, Nutt.	6⅝ x 9¾	Colorado Springs [Colorado] 1878
Townsendia exscapa, Porter	4⅛ x 6⅞	Colorado Springs [Colorado] 1878
Trifolium pratense, L. Red Clover	4⅛ x 9	Chautauqua Co. N. Y. 1870
Trifolium repens, L. White Clover	5⅞ x 9	Chautauqua Co. N. Y. 1878
Tropaeolum majus, L. Nasturtium	6 x 9	Chautauqua Co. N. Y. 1870
Utricularia inflata, Walt. (see *Prunus Persica,* L.)		
Vallota purpurea, Herb. Amaryllis	5¾ x 8⅜	Northampton [Massachusetts] 1895
Vinca minor, L. Periwinkle	6 x 8⅞	Chautauqua Co. N. Y. 1870
Viola cucullata, Ait. (see *Cyperus rivularis,* Kunth.)		
Viola Nuttallii, Pursh. Violet	6⅞ x 9¾	Colorado Springs [Colorado] 1878
Viola pedata, L. var. *lineariloba,* D. C. (see *Lonicera sempervirens,* Ait.)		
Viola pedatifida, G. Don. Violet	5⅞ x 10	Minnesota 1875
Viola scabriuscula, Schwein. Smooth Yellow Violet	5¾ x 10	Northampton [Massachusetts] 1886
Viola tricolor, L. Heart's Ease	6 x 9	Chautauqua Co. N. Y. 1870
Viola tricolor, L. Pansy	3⅝ x 7⅝	Chautauqua Co. N. Y. 1870
[Wheat with and without the awns] (see *Andropogon furcatus,* Muhl.)		
Zephyranthes rosea, Lindl. Fairy Lily	6½ x 9¾	Minnesota 1878
Zephyranthes rosea, Lindl. Fairy Lily	7⅝ x 12¼	Minnesota 1878

Emily Hitchcock Terry's Paintings of American Flowers,
enumerated by place and date[1]

Place	Date	Number
Colorado	1878	18
Florida	1875, 1876, 1878, 1879	7 [8][2]
Massachusetts	1850, 1854, 1867–70, 1879, 1886, 1890, 1892, 1895	22
Minnesota	1875–80	50 [49][2]
New Hampshire	1868	1
New Jersey	1883	1
New York	1866, 1870, 1878	18
Ohio	1883	1
South Carolina	1881	13
Vermont	1892, 1893, 1895, 1900, 1910	10

[1] Place and date not indicated on one painting.

[2] One painting is clearly misattributed to Minnesota; the species shown indicate Florida as the probable source. The numbers in brackets reflect adjustment for this error.

Plant Species Illustrated in Emily Hitchcock Terry's Paintings of American Flowers,

arranged according to place

Place	Scientific name	Common name	Date
Colorado			
Colorado Springs	*Anemone patens*, L.	Pasque Flower	1878
	Anogra albicaulis, Pursh.	White Evening Primrose	1878
	Arctostaphylos Uva-ursi, L.	Bearberry	1878
	Bossekia deliciosa, A. Nels.	False Raspberry	1878
	Castilleja integra	Painted Cup	1878
	Clematis pseudoalpina, A. Nels.	Clematis	1878, 1878
	Erigeron uniflorus, L.	Erigeron/Fleabane	1878
	Lathyrus ornatus, Nutt.	[not given]	1878
	Leucocrinum montanum, Nutt.	White Mountain Lily	1878
	Mertensia cynoglossoides, Greene	Lungwort	1878
	Oxytropis Lamberti, Pursh.	[not given]	1878
	Pentstemon angustifolius, Pursh.	Blue Beard-Tongue	1878
	Psoralea argophylla, Pursh.	[not given]	1878
	Scutellaria Brittonii, Porter	Skullcap	1878
	Thermopsis rhombifolia, Nutt.	[not given]	1878
	Townsendia exscapa, Porter	[not given]	1878
	Viola Nuttallii, Pursh.	Violet	1878
Florida			
[not given]	*Pogonia divaricata*, R. Br.	[not given]	1875
St. Augustine	*Bignonia capreolata*, L.	Cross-vine	1879
	Gelsemium sempervirens, Ait.	Yellow Jessamine	1878
	Punica Granatum, L.	Pomegranate	1876
	Rosa laevigata, Michx.	Cherokee Rose	1876
	Sarracenia flava, L.	Trumpets	1878
	Tecoma jasminoides, Lindl.	[not given]	1878
Massachusetts			
Amherst	*Allamanda Williamsi*	Allamanda	1870
	Aplectrum hyemale, Nutt.	[not given]	1850
	Caltha palustris, L.	Marsh Marigold	1870
	Castilleia coccinea, Spreng.	Painted Cup	1870
	Clematis Viticella, L.	Cultivated Clematis	1870
	Cypripedium parviflorum, var. *pubescens*, Knight	Larger Yellow Lady's Slipper	1870

Place	Scientific name	Common name	Date
Amherst (continued)	*Gentiana crinita*, Froel.	Fringed Gentian	[not given]
	Hibiscus Rosa-Sinensis, L.	Rose of China	1870
	Lilium philadelphicum, L.	Wild Orange-red Lily	1870
	Lilium superbum, L.	Turk's Cap Lily	1868
	Lobelia cardinalis, L.	Cardinal Flower	[not given]
	Pogonia verticillata, Nutt.	[not given]	1854
	Rhus glabra, L.	Sumach	1869
Cummington	[not given]	[Apple—fruit]	1867
Northampton	*Anemonella thalictroides*, L.	Rue Anemone	1895
	Aquilegia Canadensis, L.	Columbine	1879
	Cyclamen Europaeum, L.	Cyclamen	1890
	Cypripedium acaule, Ait.	Stemless Lady's Slipper	1886
	Erigeron annuus, L.	Fleabane	1890
	Erigeron Philadelphicus, L. (pink)	[not given]	1892
	Erigeron pulchellus, Michx. (blue)	Robin's Plantain	1892
	Hippeastrum Johnsoni	Amaryllis	1879
	Vallota purpurea, Herb.	Amaryllis	1895
	Viola scabriuscula, Schwein.	Smooth Yellow Violet	1886

Minnesota

Place	Scientific name	Common name	Date
[not given]	*Allium stellatum*, Ker.	Wild Onion	1878
	Anemone patens, L.	Pasque Flower	1875
	Arethusa bulbosa, L.	Arethusa	1877
	Asarum Canadense, L.	Wild Ginger	1876
	Asperula orientalis, Boiss and Hohen.	[not given]	1875
	Aster [sp.]	[not given]	1878
	Betula lenta, L.	Black Birch	1878
	Boltonia [sp.]	[not given]	1878
	Boltonia latisquama, Gray	[not given]	1876
	Bouteloua curtipendula, Michx.	[not given]	1878
	Bouteloua hirsuta, Lag.	[not given]	1878
	Bouteloua oligostachya, Nutt.	Mesquite Grass	1878
	Bromus secalinus, L.	[not given]	1878
	Cacalia coccinea, L.	Tassel Flower	1876
	Calopogon pulchellus, R. Br.	Grass Pink	1878
	Carex stricta, Lam.	[not given]	1878
	Chrysanthemum Leucanthemum, L.	Ox-eye Daisy	1878
	Cirsium discolor, Muhl.	Thistle	1875
	Cirsium muticum, Michx.	Thistle	1875
	Coreopsis lanceolata, L.	[not given]	1878

Place	Scientific name	Common name	Date
[not given] (continued)	Cynodon Dactylon, L.	Bermuda Grass	1878
	Cyperus esculentus, L.	[not given]	1878
	Cyperus rivularis, Kunth.	[not given]	1878, 1880
	Cypripedium candidum, Muhl.	Small White Lady's Slipper	1878
	Cypripedium hirsutum, Mill.	Showy Lady's Slipper	1875, 1878 1878
	Cypripedium parviflorum, var. pubescens, Knight	Larger Yellow Lady's Slipper	1875
	Erythronium albidum, Nutt.	White Dog-tooth Violet	1876
	Festuca elatior, L.	[not given]	1879
	Festuca octoflora, Walt.	[not given]	1879
	Fragaria Virginiana, Duchesne	Wild Strawberry	1875
	Gentiana Andrewsii, Griseb.	Closed Gentian	1878
	Gentiana crinita, Froel.	Fringed Gentian	1878
	Gentiana puberula, Michx.	Gentian	1876
	Gentiana quinquefolia, L.	[not given]	1878
	Habenaria leucophaea, Nutt.	Rein Orchis	1875
	Helianthus Maximiliani, Schrad.	Wild Sunflower	1878
	Hibiscus militaris, Cav.	Halberd-leaved Rose Mallow	1878
	Hordeum jubatum, L.	[not given]	1878
	Hypoxis hirsuta, L.	Star Grass	1875
	Lobelia cardinalis, L.	Cardinal Flower	1878
	Lobelia syphilitica, L.	Great Blue Lobelia	1878
	Lycium halimifolium, Mill.	Matrimony Vine	1878
	Malus Ioensis, Bailey	Wild Apple	1878
	Parnassia palustris, L.	Grass of Parnassus	1875, 1878
	Petalostemum purpureum, Rydb.	Prairie Clover	1876, 1878
	Pinguicula vulgaris, L.	Butterwort	1876
	Pogonia ophioglossoides, Ker.	[not given]	1876
	Populus deltoides, Marsh	Cotton-wood	1878
	Potentilla palustris, L.	[not given]	1878
	Prunus Persica, L.*	Peach	1878
	Ranunculus rhomboideus, Goldie	Dwarf Buttercup	1875
	Rhus glabra, L.	Sumach	1878
	Rubus idaeus	Wild Red Raspberry	1878
	Sagittaria latifolia, Willd.	Arrowhead	1875
	Scirpus sp.	[not given]	1878
	Sisyrinchium gramineum, Curtis	Blue-eyed Grass	1875
	Smilacina racemosa, L.	[not given]	1878

*Misattributed to Minnesota; probably Florida.

Place	Scientific name	Common name	Date
[not given] (continued)	*Utricularia inflata*, Walt.*	Bladderwort	1878
	Viola pedatifida, G. Don.	Violet	1875
	Zephyranthes rosea, Lindl.	Fairy Lily	1878, 1878
Clearwater	*Cypripedium arietinum*, R. Br.	Ram's-head Moccasin Flower	1878
Lake Park	*Viola cucullata*, Ait.	Blue Violet	1880
Minneapolis	*Pentstemon grandiflorus*, Nutt.	Beard Tongue	1875
New Hampshire			
Bethlehem	[not given]	Lichens, ferns, and other species	1868
New Jersey			
Orange	*Cornus florida*, L.	Dogwood	1883
New York			
Chautauqua County	*Aster puniceus*, L.	Purple Aster	1870
	Bidens cernua, L.	Bur Marigold	1870
	Campanula rotundifolia, L.	Harebell	1870
	[not given]	Clover, A Four-leaved	1870
	Convolvulus sepium, L.	Hedge Bindweed	1870
	Ipomoea purpurea, L.	Morning Glory	1870
	Papaver glaucum, Boiss.	Poppy	1870
	Ranunculus acris, L.	Buttercups	1870
	Rhododendron nudiflorum, L.	Swamp Pink	1870
	Trifolium pratense, L.	Red Clover	1870
	Trifolium repens, L.	White Clover	1878
	Tropaeolum majus, L.	Nasturtium	1870
	Vinca minor, L.	Periwinkle	1870
	Viola tricolor, L.	Heart's Ease	1870
	Viola tricolor, L.	Pansy	1870
Cooper Institute	[not given]	[Apple flower buds]	1866/1867
	Camellia Japonica, L.	[not given]	1866
	Chrysanthemum Indicum	[not given]	1866
Ohio			
Painesville	*Tecoma radicans*, L.	Trumpet Flower	1883
South Carolina			
Aiken	*Asarum arifolium*, Michx.	Wild Ginger	1881
	Deutzia scabra, Thunb.	Deutzia	1881

*Misattributed to Minnesota; probably Florida.

Place	Scientific name	Common name	Date
Aiken *(continued)*	*Dichromena latifolia,* Baldw.	[not given]	1881
	Gelsemium sempervirens, Ait.	Yellow Jessamine	1881, 1881
	Iris verna, L.	Dwarf Iris	1881
	Lonicera sempervirens, L.	Trumpet Honeysuckle	1881, 1881
	Passiflora lutea, L.	Passion Flower	1881
	Plumbago Capensis, Thunb.	Leadwort	1881
	Polygala polygama, Walt.	[not given]	1881
	Pyrus Japonica, Thunb.	Japanese Pear	1881
	Schrankia uncinata, Willd.	Sensitive Brier	1881
	Tephrosia Virginiana, L.	Goat's Rue	1881
	Viola pedata, L. var. *lineariloba,* D. C.	Bird-foot Violet	1881
Vermont			
[not given]	*Fagus grandifolia,* Ehrb.	Beech	1900
	Gentiana Andrewsii, Griseb.	Closed Gentian	1900
Bennington	*Rhinanthus Crista-galli* L.	Rattle box	1910
Dorset	*Actaea rubra,* Willd.	Red Baneberry	1893
	Campanula rotundifolia, L.	Harebell	1900
	Centaurea Cyanus, L.	Bachelor's Buttons	1893
	Coreopsis tinctoria, Nutt.	Coreopsis	1895
	Eriophorum callitrix, Cham.	Cotton Grass	1900
	Lathyrus odoratus, L.	Sweet Peas	1892
	Melilotus alba, Desr.	Sweet Clover	1895
	Papaver Rhoeas, L.	Corn Poppy	1900
Place not given			
	Andropogon furcatus, Muhl.	[not given]	[not given]
	Bromus ciliatus, L.	[not given]	[not given]
	Chrysopogon nutans, Benth.	[not given]	[not given]
	[not given]	Wheat with and without awns	[not given]

Index